The Top Dog Advantage

Books by Diane Goodspeed

Family Friendly Biking in New Jersey and Eastern Pennsylvania

Happy Tails Across New Jersey:
Things to See and Do with Your Dog in the Garden State

Agility Training for You and Your Dog

The Top Dog Advantage

Mental Management Tools and Techniques
for Competitors in Dog Sports

Diane Goodspeed

Agility & Beyond Publications

Agility & Beyond Publications
3 Blue Grass Lane
Hackettstown, NJ 07840

Library of Congress Cataloging-in-Publication Data is available
ISBN 978-0-692-20742-0

Book design by Kathleen Oswald

Photographs by Kathleen Oswald & Diane Goodspeed

Printed in the United States of America

For all the students and friends whom we have had the privilege to work with and learn from.

Contents

Demon – 2006 Training in the yard

The Beginning

My trip into the world of sport psychology began in 2006. Demon and I qualified for the American Kennel Club (AKC) Agility Nationals, which were held that year in Tampa. The event was in mid-January and I trekked down to Florida with a four-year-old dog, a tolerant husband, and two kids who were happily missing a week of school. Kevin was twelve and Kathleen was a few months short of nine-years-old. The last big event I attended was the 2000 AKC Agility Nationals. So, it had been quite a few years since I competed at a national-level competition. Add in the stress of traveling in the middle of winter with the whole family and I found myself in a permanent state of panic and anxiety while traveling south from New Jersey.

Fortunately, we had a fabulous trip and event. Demon and I put down five consecutive clean rounds and ended the event in 25th for the sixteen-inch division. I was thrilled that he came through with a solid performance in each round, despite being terrified of the crowd noises, hating the slippery floors in/out of the Tampa Convention Center, and refusing (nose up) to even step on the sod laid out for a potty area. By Sunday afternoon, I was confident that Demon and I had the skills for National competition and he had enough enthusiasm for agility to work through his worried moments and to run with focus.

My travel and training partner, Linda Brennan, did equally well with Maddie, her young Welsh Springer spaniel, and my husband and I survived the weeklong trip with two squirrely kids. Neither Kathleen nor Kevin was much interested in agility back then and spent most of the weekend playing their Game Boys or wandering around the vendor areas. On Sunday afternoon, we were all tired but happy. And then, I made a discovery that changed my perspective and my competitive career.

Again, we must go back in time for a bit. From the age of eleven and on into my first year at college, I was a competitive swimmer. When I was a sophomore, my high school team won the Illinois State Championship. Swimming from competitions to water polo to water ballet to scuba diving was pretty much year round and this was my normal for about eight years. This was well before ESPN, however, so swimming was only on TV during the Olympics. Like every other water rat, I was very familiar with Greg Louganis, who won a silver medal at the 1976 Summer Olympics and went on after the boycotted 1980 event to win two gold medals at the 1984 Summer Olympics in Los Angeles, California. Fast forward a couple decades to 2006 and I discovered Greg Louganis in Tampa at the AKC Agility Nationals. It was a frequent topic of conversation at the event: how Greg had just started training in agility and had earned multiple titles in eight months on his way to qualifying for Nationals. He had an awesome event and made the Finals with his little Jack Russell terrier, Nipper.

Success is not final, failure is not fatal.
It is the courage to continue that counts.
~Winston Churchill

Having followed his diving career, it wasn't a surprise to me that Greg Louganis would be a great competitor. However, in 2006, I had been training and competing with my dogs for almost fifteen years. I had competed with three different breeds in four sports and was already teaching agility to a wide variety of students. I had a pretty strong feeling that I knew more about agility than Greg Louganis. He, however, was in the Finals and I was packing the car!

And so began my quest....what did Greg Louganis bring to the sport that I didn't have? What skills did he transfer from diving to dog agility that beat competitors with many more years of experience in dog training and competing?

The answer to those questions is this book. The material is a compilation of what I learned and what I now use every day for myself and with all my students. It explores what I learned about mental management techniques. It took a few years to discover what skills I needed to acquire and what techniques work in dog sports. Eventually, this knowledge became part of my regular training sessions, discussions, and operating procedures in practice and at trials.

Throughout the entire learning process, I had a partner and sounding board for ideas and different techniques. My daughter, Kathleen Oswald, was always willing to experiment and test new thought. We explored most of these concepts and ideas together as her interest in agility grew.

Jenna – Training weave entries in the yard

All our dreams can come true, if we have
the courage to pursue them.
~ Walt Disney

Dare to Dream

The difference between a dream and fantasy is commitment.

Ever been enchanted by words? Magical little things aren't they? Feelings, promises, the future, the past, the present, all can be described with words. Although sometimes the words that come to mind aren't favorable, they still have meaning. And believing someone's idea, even if you don't feel it completely just because of the way they worded it…making it seem so wonderful you wish, hope, and believe what they are saying could happen. Is it all make-believe? A figment of your imagination, a simple fantasy you've conjured up? The only way to find out is to try. If you really wanted it in the first place, you'll get up and move and never turn your back on your journey or your dream.

Okay yes small pep talk from Kathleen, not important without some sort of back story. At the end of every year Diane and I plan out our goals for the months and years to follow. The obvious: attend nationals, attend tryouts, and do well, are always first on the list. After that we hit a period of silence, not an awkward one…more of a quiet thinking reflecting time, the quiet you don't interrupt to say just anything. Then Diane started to fill my mind with goals, possibilities, and a future I have dreamed of for a long time. I don't take my mother to be one for telling fairy tales, so there must have been some truth behind the future she described. I think she and I are finally on the same page, mostly about Whimzy's career (Jenna and I haven't changed much as a team). I believe Diane knows what our fate is even though I have only the faintest idea.

Agility & Beyond - Kathleen Oswald - December 31, 2011

Demon – 2012 European Open in Sweden

Introduction

In order to gain a competitive edge, athletes train for countless hours to enhance strength and speed. They hone their skills. They work on flexibility, balance and muscle control. They practice daily and compete weekly. Yet, while their endeavors frequently produce results, they do not propel the athlete from competitor to winner to champion. Something is still missing. The final component of a champion – the winning edge - is still elusively out of reach.

Your personal goal does not need to be a national championship for this to be an issue. Athletes at every level, in every sport reach a plateau of success and get stuck. There comes a point where more practice, a different trainer, new methods, a new dog, or even a different breed is not the answer. In order to improve, to be confident in every trial or test, you must search beyond the physical realm. The solution is in your head.

In order to truly excel as a competitive athlete you must condition and train your mind as much – if not more than – you train your body and canine partner. The advantage of the "top dog" in every sport is the mastery of the athlete's thinking and emotions. Your mind must be exercised and challenged just like your muscles. With training, your thoughts and emotions can become one of your best competitive advantages!

In every sport from baseball to football to ice skating to dog sports, the top athletes know that extraordinary performances require management of both muscle and mind. Controlling your thoughts, however, is much easier said than done, particularly at prestigious tournaments and events. The positive, confident flow of thoughts necessary for a best-in-class performance cannot be achieved with wishes or willpower. It is not a matter of *wanting* to control your thoughts and emotions. It is a matter of having the skills and tools to do it. For superior performances and consistency in the ring, you must know how your mind influences your body, how your body can influence your mind, how to monitor your thought processes, and most importantly, how to utilize mental conditioning techniques to stay focused on success.

Learning to use your mind can be a tremendous edge in competition. Like any other benefit though, it can only be achieved through effective training and diligent practice. It is not enough to read an occasional article on the benefits of positive thinking or to give yourself a pep talk as you complete your dog's warm-up exercises. Your dog's faultless front, zippy about turn, or gorgeous figure-8 needs consistent work and reinforcement. The same is true for your mental processes. They need the same constant refining and enhancing.

Baseball is 90% mental.
The other half is physical.
~ Yogi Berra

Adding mental training and conditioning to your daily regime is the only way to support your furry partner's best efforts in the ring every time and everywhere. Just as there are exercises to train your dog for a perfect finish, over-the-shoulder disc catch, vehicle search, or running dog walk zone, there are skills, tools and techniques that you need to learn to enhance your mental control and confidence.

Throughout my investigation of sports psychology and exploration of mental management routines and approaches, Kathleen and I have developed a process – a real method – for learning how to control your thoughts and emotions. When we teach these concepts and tools to our students, we break the overall system down into three distinct steps. Each step presents key concepts and provides specific exercises to enhance your mental mastery techniques. These are not just ideas on paper. There is very little psychological theory or big words to memorize. We leave the theory and experiments to the experts. What we present is the end result: the actual tasks and actions necessary to become the "top dog." For true success, both in competition and in life, these actions must become new life habits. From the very first set of exercises, your competitive experience will improve.

Mental mastery is a compilation of skills which build on each other and interact. The end goal is confident control - truly knowing that you can support your dog's fantastic talents and put your team's best effort into every situation and competition. As you incorporate these tools into your daily training and trialing, you will *become* the competition! And, more importantly, with confidence and emotional control, you will be able to savor every moment of competing with your best friend.

The three key components to the top dog advantage are…

Muscles over Mind System

The process begins with a discussion of how your mind and body cooperate and coordinate before, during and after an athletic competition. For optimum performances, athletes need a calm mind that lets their muscle memory programs work. This is the *muscles over mind* concept that is explored first. Our goal is to discover how the pieces that are "you" interact when you are competing and explore why your muscles (not your mind) must be in control during a competition.

Five C's of Successful Competitors

In the second section, we will explore five mental management techniques used by every successful competitor. These are the concepts and tools that make up the foundation of your new skill set. These are not just words or notions. Each of the C's has specific exercises for you to practice and incorporate into your life and competition routines.

- Calm

- Centered

- Clear Focus

- Confidence

- Control

The Competition Day

Our final step is to pull all the tools, skills and techniques together into a comprehensive program that allows you to compete with your dog at any level, anywhere and have more fun! These are concrete, real activities for you to use at a trial or an event to manage your emotions and energy level.

**Stretch break in St. Louis, Missouri, on the way to the
2012 AKC Agility Nationals in Tulsa, Oklahoma.**

**Blake Rivas's Trixie at
2013 USDAA Eastern Regional**

Muscles over Mind

As soon as sporting events existed, athletes began studying the link between mind and body. For centuries, elite athletes have tried to master the mind in order to improve their performances. The investigation of the mind-body link has been a quest for coaches, trainers and athletes at all levels of competition from pee-wee clubs to professional teams to Olympians. Many top athletes tap into and explore Eastern religions and ancient meditation techniques for help; others look to science and technology. For all, regardless of their approach, the goal is to be able to relax the mind and body to the level where optimum performances can occur.

Today, competitors have a term for the mind-body state that produces peak performances. It is more often than not referred to as *the zone*. Almost every athlete has heard of or experienced a zone performance. When competing in the zone, your mind is quiet and your body is relaxed and controlled. Within this state, the mind and body are in-sync and functioning at the highest possible level. For dog sport competitors, this magical mind-body synchronization provides the platform for perfect 200's, high-in-trial awards and national championships. When athletes master the zone, they can consistently produce fabulous performances.

Think about your last few trials. Who were the teams that you stopped to watch? Who did you make an effort to be ringside to see? Which team is always in the ribbons or on the podium? Chances are these are the handlers who frequently access and perform while in the zone. They have learned to control their thoughts and emotions and to compete at their best every time they enter the ring.

In agility, this is the handler who is able to step to the line focused one hundred percent on his dog and the course. Nothing else exists: no crowd, no rain, no judge, no tunnel traps, no clock, no other competitors. It is just the competitor and his dog against the course. Tight turns, blazing weaves, and perfect zones become the norm. Winning classes, making the Finals, and earning agility championships are commonplace events for these teams.

Across the country, this same phenomenon occurs every weekend in a dozen different canine sporting events from obedience to rally to disc dog to hunt tests to nosework and beyond. At every dog event, there are competitors who are calm and controlled and others who are nervous and jittery. Both train hard and have willing canine partners who are well trained for their event. The difference lies in the degree of mental control that the relaxed handler brings to the competition. They too may be nervous but the anxiety and nerves are under control.

Whether your goal is simply to have fun with your furry friend or win a national championship, learning how to get into the calm, anxiety free environment of the zone is well worth the effort. Being in the zone is the pinnacle of mental control. It is the master's level of thought and emotion management. Being able to shift into the zone at their choosing allows some competitors to dominate their sport for decades with multiple canine partners.

For many top-notch athletes, the zone is a normal concept and performance state. For others, it is a bit vague and elusive. Although it is a mental state that can be felt and seen, the zone is often difficult to describe - even by the best athletes and sports psychologists. What is the zone? How does a zone performance occur?

Can it truly be accessed at will? Can it be controlled? Our investigation into the zone performance phenomenon answered all of these questions and eventually led us to the first key concept of our system.

At its simplest, the zone is a peculiar state where your muscles are in control. It is a state of existence where your muscles are working over (or without) mental interference. This is the essence of the *muscles-over-mind* system.

In order to discuss the *muscles-over-mind* state further, we must delve a bit into the psychology of the mind and the physiology of the body. With a common framework, we can discuss the components that make-up who you are, how these components work together during a competition, and then explore why and how you can change and improve.

Don't think. Just do.
~Petra Ford

The Components of You

The first step is to examine how "you" are really separate components. When it comes to mental processing and thinking, "you" are not really a "you." Each of us has three distinct components:

- Conscious mind

- Subconscious mind

- Physical body

The concept of "you" as three separate pieces might be a bit strange but it is basic to psychology. Most sports psychology books separate the mind into components. The authors address the functions and interactions of the conscious and subconscious mind differently but almost all make a distinction. One of the best, Tim Galloway in *The Inner Game of Tennis* refers to the conscious mind as Self 1 (the Doer) while the subconscious mind is Self 2 (the Talker). By using two terms, Galloway easily highlights the different strengths and weaknesses of the conscious and subconscious mind and how they work during competitions. Another popular author, Lanny Bassham, also separates an individual into components in his acclaimed book, *With Winning in Mind*. He presents three concepts - conscious mind, subconscious mind, and self-image – for his discussion on mental management and excellence in sports. Both of these are excellent books with well laid out information on what makes up "you". For our discussions, we just need a few basics and a little knowledge about the mind and the brain.

Throughout an ordinary day, every activity places different demands on the conscious mind, subconscious mind and body. For example, the "you" that washes dishes, shops for groceries, reads a book, or goes to work is vastly different from the "you" that enters the ring or walks out into a field with your dog on Saturday morning. It is this difference that we need to investigate. You don't get nervous grocery shopping but you do when you setup for your first exercise in Utility. Why?

In order to answer this question, we need to look at how "you" function when competing with your dog and, like most sports psychology books, it is necessary to identify each piece and distinguish how they interact - though at a much lighter, less technical degree than a psychologist would!

Conscious mind. Your conscious mind is responsible for logic, rules and reasoning. For example, it is your conscious mind that knows you should stop for red lights, that five minus three is two, and that a snarling dog is liable to bite you. While doing its work, the conscious mind has somewhere around 50,000 thoughts (or more) per day. It is a very busy entity! Your conscious mind's ability do complex mathematics, paint a picture, surf the Internet, drive a car, and get your laundry done is all fine and absolutely necessary but you need another set of skills to win a run-off for first place at the AKC Obedience Invitational.

Neither comprehension nor learning can take place in an atmosphere of anxiety.
~ Rose Kennedy

In athletic competitions, the conscious mind has several distinct strengths and weaknesses. Five crucial aspects of the conscious mind are:

Multi-tasking. The processing power of your conscious mind can barely be duplicated by massive super-computers. It is a pro at multi-tasking. It uses dozens of inputs - both mental and physical – to maintain awareness and accomplish multiple tasks simultaneously. For instance, while typing this sentence, I am listening to a song on my I-Pod, bouncing my office chair in time to the music, and keeping track of the sheltie puppy snuffling around in the kitchen. Furthermore, while absorbing massive amounts of information, your conscious mind reasons through a gazillion possible actions to all those inputs in fractions of seconds. For example, at the end of the last sentence my conscious mind decided that the noises coming from the kitchen required immediate investigation!

Single-tasking. In today's high-tech, information-driven world, your mind rarely uses its single-tasking ability, which often leaves this valuable tool a bit rusty. The processing speed and flexibility of the conscious mind can be a powerful tool. However, the modern mind's training to multi-task is not always a strength for competitive athletes. They must also be able to focus on a single task with great intensity in order to excel at their sport.

Imagination. Your conscious mind can compute and dream up multiple outcomes for every action and situation. It effortlessly determines dozens of possible results from each action that you might take. Your imagination is an incredibly powerful asset but it works both ways. It can be an advantage or a disadvantage.

Consider Mozart, Benjamin Franklin, Monet, Thomas Edison, George Lucas, Steve Jobs, Mark Zuckerberg…their imaginations literally changed the world. Harnessing his or her imagination is a huge advantage for the competitive athlete who can use it wisely and with intent. Unfortunately, for some, their imaginations work against their best interests. They have minds that run amok with dire thoughts and disaster mini-movies. Rather than picture their trip to Westminster as a wonderful experience that nets their dog a huge trophy on Tuesday night, they see the event as an Amityville Horror sequel. They picture trips, slips, wardrobe malfunctions, hostile crowds, lost or broken equipment and a distracted, tired dog in the ring. For minds that enjoy doom and gloom scenarios, a flexible imagination is a definite weakness. Unless you are Stephan King, letting your mind create negative outcomes - vs positive, successful results - is not beneficial.

We explore this concept further in a later chapter to be sure your imagination works for you.

Verbal communication. The conscious mind thinks in words. This gives you the ability to distinguish between goal meaning to score in soccer and goal meaning an abstract idea of completing a task that you set for yourself. This is not specifically a strength or weakness. It is just something that you should be aware. The conscious mind's focus on words has a large impact on its ability to communicate with your subconscious mind.

Realize deeply that the present moment is all you ever have. Make the Now your primary focus of your life.
~Eckhart Tolle

Subconscious mind. Functioning just below your conscious mind is your subconscious mind. It is responsible for keeping track of your body's basic functions, such as digestion and breathing, and all your body's motions from sneezing to nodding to hand clapping to grooming your dog to dancing the Rumba. A large part of the *muscles-over-mind* program is to enable and reinforce your subconscious mind's abilities during an athletic competition.

The subconscious mind has several distinct strengths that are important for athletes.

Muscle memory. It is the subconscious mind that learns how to move a muscle set and then memorizes that motion for future use. These memorized motions are what Kathleen and I refer to as muscle-memory programs. Creating and using muscle-memory programs, like chewing gum, buttoning a shirt, stirring a pot, or line-dancing, is one of your subconscious mind's primary tasks. Think about how much processing power your conscious mind would require if you needed to actually *think through* walking every time you stood up! Muscle-memory programs allow you to talk on the phone, type an email, zip a coat, and drive a car effortlessly all day long with minimal conscious attention. Taping into the muscle-memorizing ability of your subconscious mind is a critical strength and is a requirement for an optimal athletic performance.

Imagery. Another critical characteristic of your subconscious mind is that it thinks in images or pictures. It does not have a word function. When you hear the word goal, your conscious mind has multiple choices. Your subconscious mind, however, can only picture an actual goal (verb), such as a soccer ball flying into a net or an actual hockey goal (noun) at the ice rink. Depending on your favorite sport, the word goal might invoke a different image, such as a football going thru uprights, but the point is that you are picturing an image – a thing or physical event - not a concept. This profound difference in communication methods can be tailored into a strength, but it can also be a weakness.

Deadly Duo of Won't and Don't

The image-orientation of the subconscious mind is why the words don't and won't are disastrous for mental communication. Think for a second about the interstate highway signs which in recent years have changed from, "Don't drink and drive," to "Drive sober or lose your license." The new message is much clearer to your mind!

Although the words don't and won't have meaning to your conscious mind, your subconscious mind can only pick out the image after the word. The negative in front of the image is ignored since it has no meaning. Consider this statement, "I want to lose weight, so I won't eat that Oreo cookie." Your conscious mind assumes it is communicating clearly. You will not be devouring that cookie (or the next one or the next one). Your subconscious mind, however, only gets the chocolaty good image of an Oreo cookie out of that statement! And, as it is your subconscious mind that controls digestion and eating, you have definitely increased the possibility that you are going to eat the Oreo cookie!

On the other hand, by focusing your conscious mind on positive, real images (like you wearing a swimsuit on the beach at a Sandals resort in the Caribbean), you can clearly communicate your intentions to the subconscious mind with amazing force.

For athletes, the deadly duo of won't and don't need to be monitored and eliminated. Heeling forward out of a halt saying "don't take a big step" is much more likely to produce a big step than a positive thought like "take small steps!"

Physical body. Your physical body responds to both your conscious mind and your subconscious mind. Your conscious mind can – and often does – take control of almost any physical activity from breathing to toe tapping. However, contrary to what your conscious mind wants you to believe, it is not superior for every task. Your subconscious mind does a superb job all by itself, particularly when relating to repetitive motions. Remember the conscious mind has no muscle-memory program. For many tasks, it actually works way too slow to truly direct a physical activity.

Consider a simple task like keyboarding. Look at the image of a blank keyboard from the United States. Can you identify where the twenty-six letters of the English alphabet are located?

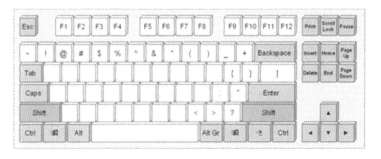

In order to identify even the most common keys, many people need to put their fingers on the keyboard and pretend to type!

When you first learned to keyboard, every letter required conscious thought. You had to picture the keyboard, find the correct key, and then move the correct finger to the right key. The learning curve was significant. This is how the conscious mind works with your body. With practice, however, most people keyboard at fifty, sixty or even one hundred words per minute. An average paragraph with one hundred words contains six to seven hundred key strokes. And yet, for an accomplished keyboarder, not a single keystroke requires conscious thought. This is how the subconscious mind works with your body. Keyboarding, like shuffling cards, braiding your hair, or riding a bicycle, is a very useful muscle-memory program.

Our brains are wired to put repetitive motions under the control of our subconscious mind. This is what muscle-memory is about and it is an incredibly important part of a *muscles-over-mind* or zone performance.

It is important to note that your body responds first to your conscious mind. It can easily interfere in the keyboarding process. This happens even to accomplished keyboarders when they encounter an unusual word (e.g., luxurious or millennium or reminiscence) or use a special character. When your conscious mind starts to think, it immediately influences how your fingers move across the keyboard. It can also happen when you add a time constraint or distraction, such as someone standing over your shoulder watching you type an email or your dog's imploring eyes begging for a walk. Furthermore, the conscious mind's interference is multiplied many times over when you are attempting a task under pressure. How many times has a heeling pattern seemed more complex during a run-off?

We are what we repeatedly do. Excellence, therefore, is not an act but a habit.
~Aristotle

The Competition "You"

So how do the three components that are "you" relate? When you are competing at an athletic event, you need all three components working in-sync. As we just noted, your conscious mind must remain calm and quiet so your subconscious mind and body can run those all important muscle-memory programs that are required for an effortless performance. This is when athletes feel they are *in the zone*. Their mind and body are calm and working together. The opposite state is pure stress.

In an agitated or excited state, your conscious mind explodes over both subconscious mind and body. Often at a competition, your conscious mind tries to grab control. It wants to think its way through the event. Thinking, however, is often not an advantage. Ever wondered about your score while you are scenting that last metal article and then flub the send? Ever feel elated over a clean run right before your dog jumps that last obstacle on an agility course and watch the bar come down? Ever think that the hard part of your disc routine is over and the rest is easy just as you over throw the next disc? Within each of these scenarios, the conscious mind is thinking when it must be quiet.

When the conscious mind thinks during a competition, bad things happen!

Capable of shifting from the present-to-past or the present-to-future in milliseconds, the conscious mind can very quickly become unruly and uncooperative. Furthermore, when the conscious mind sweeps up control, you give anxiety, fear, doubt and outrageous expectations a doorway into your head. As the conscious mind gears up, it swamps over the subconscious mind. In a micro-second all those wonderful muscle-memory programs - that took years to build - go poof! The result is a lack of coordination. Your feet stumble or you slow up one step too soon. Unknown or inappropriate verbal commands slip out. Your hands flap and fumble. On an agility course, this is often where the handler gets ahead of the course flow and skips an obstacle or just gets completely lost, unable to find the next correct obstacle.

> **The Lemon Affect**
>
> The standard example of a thought impacting your body is to think of a freshly cut lemon. Almost everyone gets a quick rush of salvia as their body responds to the image of a lemon slice. This mind-body link happens frequently – though you may not always be aware of it.

Unfortunately, your subconscious mind is not capable of shutting down a thinking conscious mind. Once it is thinking, your conscious mind sidetracks your body's basic functions. All those anxious, scary, erratic and exciting thoughts create a physiological response in your body. Your heart rate increases and your breathing changes. With your conscious mind in control, your body begins functioning on a different plane. When the judge says "Halt!" in an instant, your feet have no clue about footwork and your mouth is so dry you cannot say "Strut" to get your poor pup moving again!

Our goal is to attain equilibrium between the conscious mind, subconscious and body. Your conscious mind should be gently aware while the subconscious mind and body get the job done. In this calm, relaxed state, your subconscious mind and body can run all the muscle-memory programs that you spent hours training in practice. And, the good news is that your brain is more than capable of adopting this new state.

Success consists of going from failure to failure
without loss of enthusiasm.
~Winston Churchill

Train Your Brain

Before we can begin a program of mental mastery and control, you must believe that it is possible to change your thinking. Many athletes do not know how to change their thoughts but, even worse, there are those who believe they cannot change. In decades past, we frequently heard, "you cannot teach an old dog new tricks." Everyone heard it and many believed it. Today, we know this is ridiculous. With our current understanding of dog behavior and classical and operant conditioned learning (aka shaping), we teach old dogs new tricks all the time. If dogs can learn throughout their lives, then certainly humans can also.

Brain basics. Everything you accomplish, plan, feel and dream is governed by your brain. Weighing in around three pounds and with the consistency of warm butter, the human brain contains roughly 100 billion neurons and those neurons sole purpose is communication.

Neurons consist of a long protoplasmic fiber (axon) that conducts information away from the cell body and multiple, smaller dendrites that receive information from other nerve cells. Each point of connection between two neurons is termed a synapse. Any given neuron, particularly those in the prefrontal cortex (the part of your brain which controls executive functions like making choices, predicting future events, and governing social control), can have roughly ten thousand synaptic connections per neuron. A cubic millimeter of cerebral cortex can contain almost one billion synapses. Bottom line, you have a lot of thinking power stashed up there in your cranium!

At birth our genes lay down a basic roadmap for our neural development, including the major "highways" needed to link the functional areas of the brain. As infants, we have a framework that starts each neuron off with roughly twenty-five hundred connections. Then our exposure to the world and our experiences in it generate a more complex network of connections. These smaller, denser connections (similar to avenues and side roads) make the transfer of information between neurons more efficient and rich. By the terrible twos, sensory stimulation (aka your life experiences) has expanded the neural template in your brain to around fifteen thousand synapses per neuron. This number declines somewhat into adulthood, as many of the more ineffective or rarely used connections – like those formed singing along with Barney -- are done away with. So, as you can see, your brain has been changing for the better since your birth day.

Neuroplasticity. The point behind this biology lesson is simple: your brain is not hard-wired. It is adaptive, malleable – constantly in a state of flux. The ability of the brain to reorganize its neural connections is referred to as neuroplasticity. According to the theory of neuroplasticity, thinking, learning and acting actually change both the brain's physical structure and its functional organization from top to bottom *throughout life*. This special characteristic allows the brain to constantly lay down new pathways and to rearrange existing ones. Furthermore, most neuroscientists now agree that the human brain generates entirely new brain cells well into our golden years. While this neural regeneration was once believed impossible after age three or four, research now shows that new neurons develop constantly if a brain is challenged by and engaged in a variety of new experiences.

The brain's neuroplasticity functions in multiple ways. First, underutilized connections are deleted or weakened through a process referred to as synaptic pruning. This neural network clean-up happens constantly and is basically the brain's method for retaining active memory space. Second, neuroplasticity works to strengthen high volume neural connections. Thus, information accessed frequently gets a direct route (a straighter, wider road). So, we must not only use it to keep it but what we use gets kept and gets stronger. And, finally, neuroplasticity enables the creation of new connections. Learning new skills activates large collections of neurons simultaneously. The more neurons activated, the better we remember. Learning new information or activities increases overall synaptic density. The old adage is true. You must continue to learn for a healthy brain.

Rewire for change. The key concept here is that what you use gets reinforced and supported by more connections. So, if you upload photos to your Facebook account each week, you will effortlessly remember the sequence of steps. Stop for a few months or longer and you might need to reread the directions. This same rule applies to all your thinking patterns and the implications are huge for anyone who is seeking to change the way they think. If you consistently fire up negative thought pathways, they are truly more powerful than your positive pathways. Applying the concepts of neuroplasticity to our goal of mental control results in the following crucial ideas:

1 - When negative thoughts predominate, they get wired and supported by lots of connections. In other words, they're primed and ready to fire.

2 - Although they may be dense and efficient, these negative pathways are not permanent. The brain will rewire and disconnect them when they are no longer used.

3 - Positive thought pathways can be created and, when reinforced with consistent use, will strengthen throughout your life.

The brain's efficiency and adaptability is absolutely marvelous. As trainers, we use this in our dog's training all the time. What our dog does over and over becomes an ingrained habit. The desired behavior is produced consistently, even when under stress. We teach a behavior, proof it, and then intermittently reinforce that behavior during the dog's competitive career. This same rule applies to you! As you learn new ways to think and act, you can change your life habits forever. Our first step in this new process is to learn how to let your muscles do the work - not your mind.

Betsy Scappichio & Dealer – AKC Obedience Invitational

Cathy Brooks & Eastman – AKC Rally National
Harrisburg, PA

5 C's of Successful Competitors

Every successful mental management program or system has the same basic components. The difference is in how the common actions and attitudes are categorized. We've selected five board categories to focus on. All five are critical to monitoring and managing your thoughts and emotions but they can all be developed individually and at your own pace. With that in mind, you do not need to test yourself as you work through the sections. Just explore each of the five C's and note their interactions. We frequently find that our students come into the program with more competence at one than another. As you work the tools presented within the C, you can determine if it is a skill you already possess or one you need to strengthen.

#1 – Calm

A calm mind is necessary for the muscles-over-mind system to work. Before any competition, seminar or high-level practice, you must first calm your mind. Fortunately, the mind is as easily influenced by the body as the body is by the mind. Thus, reversing the process – deliberately using your body to control your mind – you can calm and relax your thoughts and emotions at will.

This section examines how you can use all five senses and a few key breathing exercises to influence how your conscious mind behaves. Breathing is a unique pathway to a calm mind. Breathing is the only body function that is under conscious control. Think about it, you cannot modify your digestion rate, hair growth, or pituitary gland secretions. Only breathing (or not breathing) is under your conscious mind's control. As such, breathing is a wonderful tool for connecting the body to mind.

In the same manner, all five senses are conduits. They link the outside world to your body and ultimately to your mind. Thus, each sense offers a way to manipulate your conscious mind.

So, in this section we explore all of the following:

- Breathing

- Aromatherapy

- Music

- Nutrition

- Color

- Touch

> Every human has four endowments: self-awareness, conscience, independent will and creative imagination. These give us the ultimate human freedom...the power to choose, to respond, to change.
> ~Stephen R. Covey

#2 – Centered

Once your mind is calm, it needs to be *centered* or anchored in the present moment. A quiet, centered mind simply exists. It is aware but does not judge. There is no good or bad to a mind anchored in the present moment. Things just are as they are. This is all very zen but it is true and extremely useful for athletes. Your mind resists staying in the present moment. It prefers to dwell in the past or leap about in the future! In fact, the entire discipline of meditation is aimed at holding the conscious mind in the present moment. While it isn't necessary to become a meditation expert, athletes can only compete successfully in the present. So, it is important to develop tools to manage your conscious mind to both move it into the current moment and then keep it there.

#3 - Clear Focus

With the mind calm and centered in the present, your conscious mind is now free to focus solely on one thing with great intensity. This can be a bit dangerous, especially if your mind likes doom-and-gloom scenarios! Your focus must be set clearly on success. This is also where don't and won't become most deadly. A conscious mind primed to focus is powerful so you need the tools to give it a positive, energy-enhancing focus point.

#4 – Confidence

A successful athlete is confident. This is not a word. It is a feeling, a state-of-mind. Being confident means you believe in your own ability to get things done. Confidence does not ignore fear; it takes fear apart and neutralizes it. Building confidence is a process not a task. It must be part of your overall plan. The path to confidence is not paved with a few pep talks or inspiring posters. You must build a foundation that supports successful efforts and lets you bounce back from errors or mistakes with enthusiasm and renewed energy.

#5 – Control

The last C is the compilation of the efforts from the first four. When you control your mind and are calm, you have energy control. When you maintain a stable energy level, you can manage your emotions. Emotion control gives you thought control. With energy, emotion and thought control, you can achieve anything!

Choose Happiness

People always say, "Beauty is in the eye of the beholder." I think happiness is too. There is no outline for happiness. Its definition- the quality or state of being happy - is really rather vague and open for interpretation. The state of being happy isn't determined by what others think. I believe it is the moment when you can look around and say you are proud to be where you are. You can accept all the bad, all the hurt, all the rough times because they got you to where you are today.

Happiness is beyond contentment. Contentment is satisfactory. It's easy. It's complacent. It means you are unaware of the possibilities in life. Purgatory perhaps for those living but who are not alive. Happiness is taking life into your own hands, forcing yourself sometimes to just deal with what comes your way and taking as much from every moment as you can. Because in the end, happiness isn't a feeling, it's a choice.

The choice to keep moving.
The choice to learn something new.
The choice to see all the good over the bad.
The choice to make something of everyday and every moment.
The choice to be you.

Agility & Beyond Blog - Kathleen Oswald - January 21, 2014

Most folks are as happy as they
make up their minds to be.
~Abraham Lincoln

**Betsy Scappichio & Rev – AKC Obedience Nationals
Harrisburg, PA**

#1
Calm Mind

The first "C" of success for every canine competitor is to achieve a calm, relaxed mind. Achieving a calm mind, however, can be more than a little difficult. Calm is a transient state on an average day. For the handler heading to the start line in Jumpers for the last double-Q on her first MACH, calm is as far away as a ten million dollar winning lottery ticket! On this day, when you truly need to perform your best, you probably spent most of the afternoon wondering why you didn't take up golf. And yet, you need tight lines and clean weaves for that one last qualifying score. You must calm down and relax so your dog can be awesome. Obviously, calm is much easier said than done or there wouldn't be so many discussions, articles and books about it.

A few key points about calm...

You cannot think yourself calm. It is impossible to order yourself to be calm. Assuming even that you momentarily achieve calm, it will disappear immediately when stress levels rise again. A calm mind requires fewer thoughts not more. Not only does tension cause nerves, it also causes all sorts of odd thoughts to explode into existence and many of these frequently defy logic. How could you ever be in the ring in fuzzy pink slippers? These are the thoughts that need abolishing. And yet, delving into your mind to control your thoughts is like herding puppies - corner one and two squirm away and then another escapes completely!

You cannot talk yourself calm. It is impossible to have a rational conversation with your mind once it has gone into anxiety mode. Similarly, you cannot get much across to an excited, overly stimulated mind. It likes being ecstatic and doesn't want to hear from you! You can say, "I am calm," for hours and never come close to the calm needed for a top-notch Utility test that can score a 199 or higher. If you are trying to talk yourself into calm, then we can guarantee that a relaxed mind is exactly what you are missing when you step into the ring.

Calm is a transient state. Being able to relax and calm your mind is possible. However, it is not a state in which your mind tends to remain. It'll pretty much pick any excuse to get back into its comfort zone and unfortunately, calm is not the average person's most comfortable state. Watch TV for a few hours. Calm is not modeled much in today's population. Hyper, aggravated, annoyed and excited – these are now normal. While working toward a calm mind, you'll need constant practice until it feels more comfortable and lasts longer than your average pet food commercial.

Competitions make calm harder. On trial days, at a high-powered seminar, or even just in class with a friend or family member visiting, your mind is even more unruly – producing anxious thoughts and little bursts of distracting nerves to keep you on edge or just awkward. You suddenly feel completely unprepared and extra thoughts run rampant though your mind. Heeling patterns become impossibly difficult. You are absolutely convinced your dog won't work the article pile with the judge that close. Footwork is a term your feet no longer comprehend. The Signal exercise seems hopelessly preposterous and your arm motions feel stilted. A hostile crowd seems to be forming just as you finish your warm-up. And, the mere thought of a run-off has your nerves jumping and jerking like a cat on a short leash walking through the dog pound.

And, to make it all worse, our canine partners *always* key into these feelings of anxiety and tension and inevitably our fears prove true. The practice, run or test falls apart when your internal tension leads to a squeaky voice and tight muscles. Within that state, we tend to use the wrong verbal command or it just sounds wrong to our furry partner. Motions become erratic and twitchy. Bad thoughts generate bad movements. On the flip side, good thoughts produce solid, good movements!

Trust yourself. Create the kind of self that you will be happy to live with all your life. Make the most of yourself by fanning the tiny, inner spark of possibility into flames of achievement.
~Golda Meir

So how do we achieve calm?

You cannot control your mind but you can take charge of your body. By relaxing your body, you can gain control of your thoughts. Obviously our minds and bodies are intricately linked. Where your mind goes your body follows. Think of a fresh cut lemon slice or candy lemon drop. Feel your mouth produce extra saliva? Perhaps you can even smell the lemon scent? This is your mind producing a physical change in your body with mere thought. And, because your mind and body are connected, you can reverse the process.

You can use your body to alter your mental state.

In every practice session, handlers train their dogs and their own bodies for control. Being aware of your body – from shoulder and hip alignment to hand and foot position - is a normal part of almost every training session. It is also an integral part of mental training.

Your mind and body always remain in-sync. If your mind is wired, your body will be. If your mind is calm, your body will be too. This is the core principle that provides access to calm. It is your doorway to peak performances.

To open the door – to use your body to control your mind – you must build awareness of your body, in particular its energy state. You must tune-in and pay attention to how your body is functioning. Asking your conscious mind about your energy state is fine when you're gently scratching your dog's ears. If you are stressed, tense, agitated or excited, asking your conscious mind for feedback is generally useless. It is much easier to simply key into your body. Although your mind may be functioning in gibberish mode, you can easily detect whether you are holding

Where the mind goes, the body follows. The reverse is also true. Where the body goes, the mind will follow.

your breath, breathing rapidly, clenching your jaw, walking stiffly, or fumbling on your own feet. Any or all of these are signposts of tension and stress.

One of our primary goals is to use the body-mind connection at trials and in competitively stressful situations. In order to do this, you need a new habit. You must constantly become aware of your body's energy state. If your internal energy level is too high, you will be distracted or agitated. You will suffer from jumpy thoughts, restlessness, forgetfulness and, of course, erratic breathing. Tension frequently appears in rigid shoulders. Anger makes us hold our breath and fear sends adrenaline pumping through your system, which jazzes up your heart rate. None of these are considered calm. If your internal energy level is too low, then you will have sluggish thought processes. You may feel lethargic or even worse, you may feel bored. Often you physical responses become weak and out of rhythm. Concentrating becomes impossible and yawning becomes its own activity.

> *You may not be able to control your mind but you can always control your body.*

Either of these states and many in between prevent you from being your best for your canine partner.

A low or high energy-level can be corrected easily with body-mind exercises and environment changes. Most trainers do this instinctively with their dogs. If our dog's energy level is too high, we send them for a run, take a brief time-out, or switch exercises. If our dog's energy level is too low, we bring out a favorite toy, swap to a higher value treat, or change to a low stress exercise. Energy state maintenance needs to be just as instinctive when applied to you.

With an enhanced awareness of your energy state, you can learn when to use the exercises and therapies presented in this chapter. All of the body-awareness exercises work in harmony and, as with you work through each one, you will become more in-tune to your body and more aware of its energy state. This improvement in awareness works for competitions and for life.

The following six methods investigate the body's connection to the mind to create or enhance a calm, relaxed state.

- Breathing

- Aromatherapy

- Music

- Nutrition

- Color

- Touch

All of the skills and exercises that we explore in each body-mind link can and should be used together. You may find one to be extremely powerful, another not so much. Some may fit easily into your competitive routine. Others you may have to work at. Try each one more than once. They are all intricately linked and form a network for body-awareness and mental control. Think of these exercises as building blocks. With each layer that you incorporate, your foundation for control gets stronger and more resilient.

Breathing

Every breath you take validates your existence. The steady inhale-exhale of life is instinctive and as natural as sleeping and waking. It begins with birth and its cessation heralds death. Furthermore, it is the only physiological system over which your mind has any control. Think about it. Most of us cannot control our heart rate, digestion, or liver functions. And, even if you learn biofeedback techniques, you most certainly cannot stop - even for a millisecond - your heart from beating or your stomach from digesting. Yet you could hold your breath right now for twenty or thirty seconds or even for a full minute. Your conscious mind can shut down, slow down or speed up one of the most vital systems in your body.

It is this unique body-mind connection that can function for you - for control. Your body constantly sends messages to the brain. If you consciously hold your breath long enough, your body will send a full stampede of messages to your mind to knock it off! However, when done with constructive purpose, breathing consciously provides is a fabulous communication link between your body and mind. Depending on age, health, body size and sleep/wake patterns, the average adult takes between twelve and twenty breaths per minute. So, we have around 20,000 opportunities a day to snag control over one of the best body-mind communication links.

With a bit of practice, you can easily use breathing to modify your heart rate, blood pressure and energy levels. All of which in turn allow you to modify thought flow and focus. Breathing truly links body, mind and spirit. For this reason, breathing exercises are integral to many Eastern religions and play an important part in yoga and many meditation practices. Without becoming a religious guru or meditation specialist, you can use breathing techniques and exercises to control stress, tension and anxiety. Even better, breathing exercises used in a competitive environment can instantly bring your mind into equilibrium and focus your thoughts on success.

Breathing consciously can

+ Change your physical state - either calm your nerves or raise your energy level

+ Set your focus - pull you inside your own mind to ignore distractions and focus on the task at hand

+ Build a trigger - achieve calmness instantly anywhere and anytime

Breath is the bridge which connects life to consciousness, which unites your body to your thoughts.
~Thich Nhat Hanh

Before we discuss breathing exercises and when to use them, it is important to understand how breathing works and what carbon dioxide and oxygen levels effect. So first, we must do a brief biology lesson.

How Respiration Works

The function of our respiratory system is to exchange two gases: oxygen and carbon dioxide. Oxygen comes in and carbon dioxide goes out. The exchange of gases takes place in the lungs, specifically in the millions of alveoli which are surrounded by blood capillaries. There are three processes involved in the transfer of oxygen from the outside air to the blood flowing to our cells: ventilation, diffusion, and perfusion. Ventilation moves air in and out of the lungs. Diffusion is the spontaneous movement of gases between cells. Perfusion is the process by which the cardiovascular system pumps blood throughout the body. For breathing exercises, we want to focus on ventilation and diffusion and then ultimately the body's use of carbon dioxide.

Ventilation. The air we inhale is roughly 78% nitrogen, 21% oxygen, 0.96% argon and 0.04% carbon dioxide, helium, water, and other gases. Your lungs cannot inhale or exhale on their own. They are more like solid sponges. It is the muscles of the rib cage, chest and diaphragm that move air in and out. Imagine that your chest is like a squat, flexible barrel with the lungs attached to the walls. The floor of the barrel is your diaphragm. It's the action of the barrel walls and floor that result in the movement of air into and out of your body. When air is sucked into the lungs, it eventually sinks to the alveoli where it contacts millions of capillaries or more specifically, the red blood cells inside the capillaries.

> *Our bodies need both oxygen and carbon dioxide to function properly.*

Diffusion. Diffusion occurs twice: once in the lungs and once in the tissues at a cellular level. Red blood cells, or more precisely the hemoglobin proteins in the red blood cell, are always in one of two states: oxygen carrying or carbon dioxide carrying. The vital exchange of carbon dioxide and oxygen happens through diffusion. For it to work, the concentration of the gases must be *different* across a permeable barrier, such as a cell wall.

In the lungs, as we inhale, we create a low carbon dioxide and high oxygen concentration gradient. This occurs naturally by breathing fresh air which has about 21% oxygen and 0.04% carbon dioxide. Oxygen travels through the lung and then diffuses into the red blood cells, which arrive at the lung in an oxygen depleted state. This is the first imbalance of oxygen/carbon dioxide that we use to breath. The oxygen loaded red blood cells then travel through the body to a cell. At the cell, there is high concentration of carbon dioxide. Again diffusion is setup naturally since a hard working cell produces plenty of carbon dioxide. Your hemoglobin loves carbon dioxide more than oxygen, so it releases the oxygen to soak up all the carbon dioxide. The oxygen moves from the blood (high concentration area) to the cell (low concentration area). Once the carbon dioxide is attached to the red blood cell, it takes a ride back to your lungs. At the lung, the carbon

> *Anaerobic respiration is without oxygen while aerobic respiration is with adequate oxygen.*

dioxide releases from the hemoglobin, due to the high oxygen concentration in the lung, and off the carbon dioxide goes into the atmosphere around your head.

Carbon dioxide. Over the last few decades carbon dioxide has received lots of bad press. Carbon dioxide in the environment might be toxic but it is actually vital to our health. *Our bodies need both oxygen and carbon dioxide.* It is the delicate balance between the two gases that allows our systems and cells to function.

Low levels of carbon dioxide can impact a huge range of physiological functions. Our cells use oxygen to efficiently produce energy. And, oxygen delivery is dictated by the concentrations of carbon dioxide throughout our bodies! Oxygen cannot move unless the appropriate concentrations of carbon dioxide are maintained. Remember hemoglobin adores carbon dioxide. In the cell where oxygen is needed most, it is the affinity for carbon dioxide that gets the oxygen released from the hemoglobin. Diffusion actually moves the oxygen into the cell. So, in a low carbon dioxide environment, oxygen just stays attached to the hemoglobin in the red blood cell. It never moves into the cell where it is desperately needed.

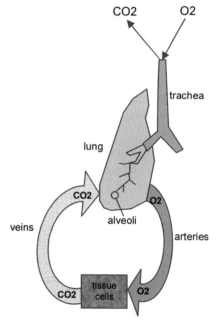

Fortunately, our bodies have an alternate system to continue functioning. In a low oxygen environment, our cells switch to anaerobic (without oxygen) respiration to produce energy. Unfortunately, anaerobic respiration produces less energy and it's by product is lactic acid versus carbon dioxide and water. Instead of being useful (as are carbon dioxide and water), lactic acid is acidic and needs to be removed. So, the point to the biology lesson – you need carbon dioxide. It keeps your cells going on aerobic respiration rather than having to switch to damaging and less efficient anaerobic respiration. The lactic acid is eventually cleaned up as the body regains normal carbon dioxide levels but this recovery takes time.

There are several other impacts from high/low carbon dioxide levels. Carbon dioxide is a smooth muscle relaxant. With high levels of carbon dioxide, the airways and the blood vessels of the circulatory system are able to relax and dilate, allowing efficient distribution of oxygen and nutrients such as glucose. This improves performance and allows aerobic energy production to continue even longer. Carbon dioxide also affects brain functions. Your brain uses four times more oxygen than any other part of your body. And, as with all cellular functions, it is carbon dioxide that controls the delivery of oxygen to the brain. Low carbon dioxide levels cause the brain to become oxygen deficient which makes it hyperactive. Humans experience this as anxiety. So, carbon dioxide is not only your muscle relaxer but your brain's natural tranquilizer.

Carbon dioxide levels are controlled by breathing. Efficient, correct breathing is critical for healthy living and clear thinking. Learning to maintain and manipulate your breathing patterns is critical to your ability to control your own calm.

Breathing Styles

We breathe an average of 20,000 times a day. A normal breathing or respiratory rate for an adult at rest is twelve to twenty breaths per minute. During exercise your respiration rate increases and when you sleep it slows. Years of sitting too much, anxious thinking, tension, and the normal pressures of living frequently result in breathing patterns that are less than ideal for competitive athletes. These bad breathing habits commonly lead to rapid, upper-chest breathing which leads to over-breathing which leads to depletion of carbon dioxide. Furthermore, emotions and breathing have a reciprocal relationship. When you are relaxed and composed, your breathing is slow and rhythmical. When you are anxious or nervous, your breathing quickens and may even become erratic. This upsets the balance between oxygen and carbon dioxide.

It is important to note that your body functions in a wide range of oxygen-carbon dioxide concentrations. It has to! Your breathing style or method determines how much oxygen or how much carbon dioxide you have in your system. Too much oxygen (relative to the level of carbon dioxide) makes most people feel agitated and breathless which causes your nervous system to go into overdrive. Too much carbon dioxide (again, relative to the level of oxygen) can leave you feeling sluggish, sleepy and tired.

With rib muscles, chest muscles and the diaphragm available to move air though the lungs, a variety of breathing styles are possible.

High-breathing. Sometimes called collarbone breathing, high-breathing involves raising the ribs, collarbone and shoulders. It is the least desirable form of breathing. High breathing is shallow and extremely inefficient. Only the upper lobes of the lungs are used, which have a small air capacity, and the greatest exchange of oxygen/carbon dioxide occurs in the lower lobes of the lungs. If you mainly use high breathing, then you are not getting oxygen to the lower lung. This forces you to breathe more rapidly in order to achieve the appropriate exchange of gases. Rapid breathing also gets rid of too much carbon dioxide.

Middle-breathing. Sometimes referred to as rib breathing, this breathing style fills the middle parts of the lungs with air. The ribs and chest expanded out or sideways and the diaphragm moves up and down. Thus, there is air flow through both the upper and lower lobs. It is useful during physical exercise.

Low-breathing. Yoga practitioners prefer diaphragmatic breathing or abdominal breathing. Low-breathing moves the abdomen in and out, changing the position of the diaphragm. It allows air to flow into the lower lobes of the lung and is usually a slower rate of breathing, which optimizes the carbon dioxide/oxygen balance. Whenever you slouch or slacken your shoulder, you normally adopt low-breathing. We often use low breathing when sleeping. However, when we are physically active, abdominal breathing is inadequate.

> **Breathing Style Test**
>
> Test your breathing style with this simple test. Sit comfortably in a chair and place your right hand on your chest and your left hand on your abdomen. Breathe normally for 30 seconds. As you breathe, notice which hand rises more. If your right hand rises more, then you are a high-breather. If your left hand rises more, then you are a diaphragm or low-breather. If both move about the same, you are a middle-breather.

If you don't like something, change it.
If you can't change it, change your attitude.
~Maya Angelou

So, to summarize this brief biology lesson and the information on breathing styles, breathing controls both oxygen and carbon dioxide levels. Carbon dioxide levels in turn control much of the physiology throughout your body. With this information, our goal is to control your breathing to alter your physiology on purpose.

Breathing Exercises

In order to control your physiology, you need to take conscious control of your breathing. By consciously controlling your breathing, you can set your body's carbon dioxide level to relax your mind and muscles and calm your emotions. Alternately, you can use breathing exercises to increase your energy and alertness. Breathing exercises are as common as diets. There are literally hundreds from which to choose. The ones we've selected for the *muscles-over-mind* system are easy to learn and incorporate well into dog sporting events. You may find one breathing exercise works better for you than another. Preferences are fine so long as you are comfortable with the exercise. Practice them all and then select the one(s) that works best for you. At a trial, you should not need to reference this book when you need to calm down!

Breathing consciously is a powerful tool for mental control. However, like any other new skill, it also requires practice. There are three steps to mastering breathing exercises:

1 - Practice in a quiet, controlled environment

2 - Use in a mildly stressful or hectic environment

3 - Incorporate into your competition routine

The goal is for you to practice these breathing exercises in a variety of situations before you need them at a trial. Breathing calmly in a flower garden is just fine for a yoga practitioner. Breathing calmly in a huge arena with dog fans still howling their delight at your competition's fabulous performance is an entirely different skill! You do need, however, to start in the garden or in a quiet room without distractions. Once the routines are easy then you can begin to use them in a variety of situations. A few minutes a day is time well spent.

Fortunately, anxiety is not limited to competitions. It can and does appear in your life pretty much daily. Stress surfaces with every deadline at work. Tension can turn up at a stoplight and multiples in traffic jams. And, for some, a dentist appointment can be as anxiety loaded as a shuttle launch. So, the next time the person in line behind you at the grocery store is humming tunelessly or an obsessive trainer in your class won't leave the go-out practice area so you can have a turn, select a breathing exercise and start practicing. Every stressful or uncomfortable situation offers you an opportunity to practice your breathing routines until your immediate response to anxious feelings, stress or tension is calm breathing. There are examples for each of the following exercises to guide you through the practice steps.

> *Use the stress and tension of everyday life to train daily for competitions.*

When you incorporate these breathing exercises into your competitive routines, they need to be second nature and easily executed. You should automatically begin one of these exercises as soon as you feel anxious or you are mired in negative thinking. Trial environments have stressors everywhere – from the cramped parking areas, to the check-in line, to the stewards that misplace your utility bag, to the competitor who needs a squeaky toy to keep her dog focused during the warm up. Some days just getting into the ring produces enough stress to send you crawling back into bed to snuggle with the cat. Once you are at a trial, however, you must handle every challenge that appears and be calm enough to let your muscle-memory programs work.

Breathing exercises are a great defense against all the difficult situations inherent in trialing – ring nerves, difficult stock, inexperienced volunteers, a hot, tired judge, wind and rain, or even a distracted or overly excited dog. Once the breathing exercises are easy and a natural response to stress, incorporating them into your trial routine is easy. You do not need to become a new-age peace and love guru. Just use one of the breathing exercises to relax your mind when you are in situations that generate stress or to raise your energy when you are too relaxed or tired.

During the learning phase, practice a few times per week. While learning, sit on a comfortable chair in a quiet room, on a blanket in the garden, or on a secluded bench in the park. Distractions should be minimal. And this includes your canine pal. Keep your pup quiet and calm while you focus on your breathing exercises. When you go quiet and calm, your dog is bound to think it would be better for you to scratch his ears or throw the ball.

For pre-competition practice, find and use everyday stressors that put you out of balance. Some common stressors that make practicing easy:

- waiting in line at the grocery store
- stuck behind a school bus on your way to work
- trapped in traffic while trying to get to your evening nosework class
- long lines during the morning rush hour at Starbucks
- supporting a friend who needs to vent (breathing keeps you from absorbing her stress which lets you offer constructive help)
- debating/arguing with family members
- waiting at the vet's office
- sitting in the dentist chair
- anxiety generated by competition thoughts

Please do not attempt these exercises if you have any breathing or heart issues. If you feel light-headed at any time, stop immediately. If you have a history of respiratory illness or disease, please consult a trained professional breathing coach or doctor before beginning.

Breathing exercises: calm and relax. Each of the first two exercises will bring you from anxious to calm first by raising your CO2 level and second by focusing your thoughts on the counting process. There are two simple exercises: 4-7-8 breathing cycles and complete breath cycles.

4-7-8 Breathing Cycles

This breathing pattern raises your CO2 level; thus it functions as a natural tranquilizer for the nervous system. You should use this exercise when you are nervous or excited. For example, if you get anxious at the mere thought of a major competition or trialing under a certain judge, use this exercise to lower your anxiety. This exercise gains power with repetition and practice. It is also a core component of the mental management routine in your competition day, which is discussed in the last section of this book.

Exercise Steps

1 - Sit with your back straight. Relax your shoulders. Close your eyes. Place your right hand on your chest and your left hand on your abdomen. Once you've become proficient with this exercise, you can simply let your hands rest comfortably in your lap.

2 - Inhale slowly, smoothly and deeply for 4 seconds. Keep your mouth closed. As you inhale, fill your lungs from bottom to top. Fill your lower lungs first; feel your left hand rise. Then fill your upper lungs; feel your right hand rise.

3 - Hold your breath for 7 seconds.

4 - Exhale slowly for 8 seconds. Exhale through an open mouth. Some people find it helpful to make a soft swoosh noise as they breathe out.

That's one breath cycle. Pause briefly and then do two more cycles of 4-7-8.

In competition, this is the perfect breathing exercise for when you are a one or two dogs away from your turn in agility, during the transition between dogs in rally or obedience, or while waiting for the stock to settle in a herding test. It raises your CO2 levels to promote relaxation and it keeps your mind focused. If you keep counting 4-7-8, then you won't be anxious about the drop-on-recall or stressed about a weave entry. While you are counting, you are controlling your breathing and your mind does not have enough computing power left to create disaster scenarios, focus on the competition, the crowd, or any other distraction!

When you own your own breath,
nobody can steal your peace.
~ author unknown

Complete Breath Cycles

Prepare for this exercise by breathing naturally for 10-15 seconds. Do not try to influence your breathing, just focus on the natural inhale/exhale process to clear your mind. For this exercise, inhale with your mouth closed and exhale with your mouth open.

Exercise Steps

1 - Inhale to fill lower abdomen (belly), middle chest, and then upper chest. As your inhale, relax the belly muscles. Feel as though the belly is filling with air. Keep inhaling. Fill up the middle of your chest. Feel your chest expand and rib cage open sideways. Keep inhaling to fill upper chest.

2 - Hold the breath in for a moment.

3 - Exhale as slowly as possible. As the air is slowly let out, relax your chest and rib cage. Begin to pull your belly in to force out the remaining breath. You may find it helpful to make a soft "humming" noise as you exhale

That is one round. Work 5 rounds in a cycle. After each cycle, check your physical state. If you are still tense or nervous, simply repeat the set. Once your start, make a commitment to completing all five breaths.

In competition, use the complete breath cycle when you need to reset your system from anxious to calm. If all the competitors ahead of you flunk the jumpers course or every dog in the class blows the down signal, your mind may go into full blown mental panic. You lose hope of qualifying and start thinking of all the other things you should be doing that day! You need to reset your mind. No one makes rational decisions while panicking. Retreat to your car or a quiet location and take a mental time out from the competition. Use one or two complete breath cycles to bring yourself back into equilibrium.

This exercise also has the effect of opening you up physically. The combination of focused breathing and slow counting does an excellent job of connecting the body and mind.

Breathing exercises: energize There are also times when you need to raise your energy level. Competition requires energy. If you are too calm or too relaxed, then you will not perform at your best. Peak performances occur when you are energized and controlling your nervous anxiety. Try one of the following exercises when your find yourself sleepy, unenthused or just plain lazy when heading into a walk-through or are warming up for your afternoon class at an obedience or rally trial.

There are two simple methods to lower your CO_2 level: bellows breathing and a Tai Chi breathing exercise.

Bellows Breathing

When you do this exercise, you will feel invigorated and recharged. Try this breathing exercise the next time you feel the need to reach for a cup of coffee. Stand up straight and keep your mouth closed. Inhale and exhale rapidly through your nose. This automatically shifts you into upper-chest breathing, which will lower your CO_2 level. Your breaths in and out should be very short and equal in duration. This is a noisy breathing exercise. You are doing it correct when you hear each breath suck in and blow out.

Exercise Steps

1 - Breath in-and-out three times very, very quickly. This produces a quick movement of the diaphragm, like a bellows.

2 - Repeat three times in rapid succession with a slight pause between sets.

3 - Breathe normally after each cycle.

Stop this exercise immediately if you feel lightheaded or woozy. After a few seconds of normal breathing, you can retry the cycle to increase your energy level.

Focusing on the act of breathing clears the mind of all daily distractions and clears our energy enabling us to better connect with the spirit within.
~ author unknown

> You can't make positive choices for the rest
> of your life without an environment that makes
> those choices easy, natural, and enjoyable.
> ~ Deepak Chopra

Tai Chi Breathing Exercise

A very fine, short breath exercise comes from the Chinese Tai Chi, which is a martial arts practice used for defense and health. The exercise uses three short inhales done through the nose and three correlated arm lifts. Again, like many breathing exercises that incorporate motion, it seeks to link your body and breathing to control your energy level. The three short intakes lower your carbon dioxide level and provide an easy energy raiser.

Exercise Steps

1 - Stand up and let your arms hang loosely at your sides.

2 - On the first inhale, lift your arms from your side straight out in front to shoulder height.

3 - On the second inhale, move arms out sideways, still at shoulder height.

4 - On the third inhale, lift arms straight over your head.

5 - Exhale through the mouth while moving your arms in an arc back down to your side.

Stop this exercise immediately if you feel lightheaded or woozy. After a few seconds of normal breathing, you can retry the cycle to increase your energy level.

Aromatherapy

Our sense of smell is insignificant compared to our dogs but our scenting ability is keener and more influential than many people realize. We tend to believe that sight and hearing are the two most critical senses for our survival. However, from an evolutionary perspective, smell is one of the most important senses and it is built into one of the oldest parts of our brain. The olfactory bulb, which converts smell information from your nose to your brain, is sometimes referred to as the "emotional brain." It is closely tied to the amygdala, which processes emotion, and the hippocampus, which is responsible for associative learning. Thus, our brains constantly connect smells to memories and then emotions to the memory. These links happens all day without your being aware of it.

Consider our ancient ancestors...those who quickly linked the musty smell of a saber-tooth cat with extreme alarm were much more likely to survive! You've been genetically engineered for millions of years to link smells with positive and negative events.

When you first encounter a new order or scent, your brain links it to an event, a person, a thing, or a specific place. For example, you might associate oil with the garage, chemical cleaners with a visit to the vet, baking bread with your grandmother's kitchen, chlorine with a pool, or a wet dog with your last hike in the rain. Once the association is built, your mind also links your emotion and your mood with that smell. This is part of the reason why everyone likes different scents. We encountered more new odors in our youth so smells are often related to childhood events and places. However, or whenever, they are created, each of us has individual memories associated with any given odor. All your life, your mind has been creating a smell database.

A smell can bring on a flood of memories, influence your mood, and can definitely affect your work and athletic performances. This is also true for your dog. You definitely have a different response to the vet office smell than your dog!

Despite the tendency of humans to underestimate the role of smell and its influence on our behavior, for most mammals smell is the most important sense. We know our dogs use their olfactory system to find toys, track, explore their environment, and communicate with each other, but we are often unaware of how scent influences our daily lives.

> Humans have about 5 million receptors for smells. Dogs have over 200 million!

The olfactory system is one of the oldest parts of the brain and it is far from dormant. Recent research has improved what we know about the olfactory system, but the fact remains that much remains to be discovered. You can, however, begin to use your sense of smell to influence your own behaviors. Smells trigger memories and emotions. And, triggers can be very useful in competitive environments *when you control them*!

Scent Selection

Some scents can make you sleepy; some more alert. Some scents will raise your confidence, while others can energize you better than a cup of espresso. With a little bit of experimenting and some practice, the mood changing ability of scents can also aid your athletic performances. You can actually sniff yourself calm or alert!

Aromatherapy is the oldest "new" therapy. Scent usage dates back thousands of years to the ancient Greeks and Romans (and probably much further). Modern aromatherapists use scents for pain reduction, digestion control, antidepressants, fever control, mood modifications, and much more. In today's global economy, we have access to dozens of unique oils that can easily and quickly alter our moods and influence behaviors. Specific scents or combinations can make you more creative, alert or calm your nerves. It is a powerful tool when used correctly and creatively and it works on both you and your dog. Humans have about 5 million receptors for smells. Dogs have over 200 million!

> *Aromatherapy is not an exact science. It is more an ongoing personal quest for knowledge about yourself.*

As with the other body-mind links, scent therapy requires that you tune into your physiological state. How do you feel? The answer – wired, tired, or somewhere in between – lets you know which scent to select and when to use it. This is the same process you go through when using the breathing exercises. All of the tools for linking your body and mind work in harmony though. Scent therapy can truly enhances the power of your breathing exercises.

Scents can be used around the house, in the car, or at work, but our ultimate goal is to get scent therapy working for you at specific points in your competitive routine. Before that can happen, we need to understand how to pick scents and how they work on your emotions.

Nothing is more memorable than a smell.
~Diane Ackerman

Scent Basics

Not all aromatherapy products are the same. When purchasing, look for essential oils not fragrance oils. Fragrance oils are often chemicals mixed to resemble popular scents and they often have an alcohol base. Essential oils are made from plant material, which can be petals, leaves, stems, roots, fruits, or seeds. The oil is extracted through cold press, steam or water distillation, or a solvent extraction process. When compared to fabricated fragrances, essential oils are highly concentrated and, in many cases, require considerable plant material to create the oil. For example, it can take up to sixty roses to create a single drop of rose oil. Thus, essential oils are also more expensive.

In order to be useful, essential oils are mixed with a carrier oil. Common oils mixed with essential oils are olive, sweet almond, sunflower, safflower or grape seed. If you have allergies, be careful to check the carrier or base oil before using an essential oil. Please check the cautions carefully before using any natural oil and always store oils in well sealed, dark bottles.

There are more than five hundred different essential oils that are recommended by aromatherapists to address health issues and adjust attitudes in their clients. In order to stay on target, the following only addresses the most common, easily obtained mood-enhancing natural oils. There are many, many more than discussed here. There are also plenty of combination products available online, at retail stores, spas and health stores. The descriptions and information we've provided is only intended to get you started. Many of the plants and their growing environments are different in various countries as are the methods used to create the oils. For example, you might enjoy lavender grown in Spain, Australia, Bulgaria, Great Britain, France, or Texas! Each has its own chemical footprint and a unique scent. Always keep in mind that reactions to smells are highly individual. Explore and decide for yourself what oils work best for you. You should test an assortment of scents around the house, in the car, or at work. Once you know which ones you enjoy, then you can add aromatherapy to your practice sessions and trial days.

In addition to the essential oils, keep in mind also the important link between scents and food. All essential oils are from plants and many are from foods that make great additions to a trial diet! For example, you can get both a nutritional boost and a touch of energizing scent therapy when you peel and eat an orange or tangerine. Another excellent source of energy is peppermint, which can be consumed as well as sniffed. Vanilla, bergamot and chamomile will be calming and relaxing. When you are selecting or baking food for competitions, keep in mind that the scent(s) in the food should also match the energy state you are trying to attain or maintain.

Traditional Chinese Medicine (TCM)

In traditional Chinese medicine, the body and mind are considered a network and must be treated and balanced as a whole. In traditional Chinese culture and medicine, every food has properties and actions and all foods are identified as warming (yang), cooling (ying) or neutral. Foods are then consumed specifically to balance the body and treat disease. No food is inherently bad or good. Foods must be used appropriately. These same basic rules can also be applied to scents. Many scents have strong warming and cooling properties. When you feel restless, uptight, or excited, you are hot or warm. Look for cooling scents and foods to rebalance. When you feel fatigued, weak or sluggish, you are cold or cool. Look for warming scents and foods to rebalance.

Calming Scents

For calming scents look for essential oils that have properties that balance the mind, calm nerves, and relieve anxiety. Many of the calming scents blend well together so you can combine scents easily to keep the odor fresh and interesting. Since you only need a few drops to scent an area, it is easy to experiment with your own mixes. Some common calming scents are:

Benzoin. This thick oil has a sweet, vanilla-like aroma, is a golden color, and comes from the tropical benzoin tree. Deep incisions are made in the trunk of the tree, from which a colored sap exudes. When the resin becomes hard and brittle, it is collected from the bark and then the resin is solvent extracted to release the benzoin oil. This resinous oil can instill confidence and enhance feelings of contentment. It blends well with wood oils, like sandalwood or cedarwood, and citrus oils, like bergamot, orange, and mandarin. Cautions: Benzene and its derivatives are highly aromatic but are toxic in nature. Do not ingestion or inhale in excess.

Bergamot. This is a calming essential oil with a fresh, lightly floral smell. Its name is derived from the Bergamo, the city in Italy, where the oil was first sold. Bergamot oil is made from a citrus tree. It is the rind from the bergamot orange that produces the oil. Bergamot is one of the most widely used essential oils in the perfumery and toiletry industry. It is also used to flavor Earl Grey teas, which makes a nice alternative to chamomile tea, when you need a calming brew. Bergamot is uplifting, balances the spirit, and reduces tension and anxiety. It blends very well with a wide variety of scents, particularly lavender, sandalwood, jasmine, Ylang-ylang, and Neroli. Caution: Bergamot oil can cause burns when used on a sensitive skin which is then exposed to sunlight.

Chamomile. An excellent calming oil, this herb is well known for its powerful sedating effect. In the form of a tea, chamomile is a marvelous relaxing drink. In aromatherapy, its properties also include pain relieving and stress reduction. Chamomile is a type of plant with daisy-like white flowers from a low-growing perennial herb. The oil is extracted from the flowers by steam distillation. There are a wide variety of chamomiles, Roman, German, Cape, etc, all of which have their own unique properties and scents. It blends well with bergamot, benzoin, sandalwood, vetiver, Ylang-ylang, ginger, lemon and frankincense. Cautions: Chamomile is a member of the ragweed family. Always test a small amount first for sensitivity or allergic reaction, particularly when experimenting with the different regional sources.

Clary sage. A clear to pale yellow essential oil, clary sage has an earthy scent with a hint of fruit. The plant is native to southern Europe and has large leaves and lilac, pale blue, pink, or white flowers. Clary sage oil is extracted by steam distillation from the flowering tops and the leaves. Although not a cheap oil, it is believed to help stimulate the body's natural production of endorphins that ease fatigue and chronic pain. It is excellent at reducing stress and balancing emotions. It blends well with almost all the calming scents. Cautions: Do not take internally or combine with alcohol. A heavy dose can cause headaches.

Eucalyptus. The best source is derived thru steam distillation of the leaves of the Eucalyptus plant. This essential oil, with its strong earthy scent, is both refreshing and calming. It has powerful antibacterial and antiviral properties and the strong camphoric element increases blood circulation. It blends well with lavender, rosemary, and thyme. Caution: May irritate sensitive skin.

Frankincense. A firm favorite in aromatherapy for thousands of years, this essential oil has a woody, sweet aroma with a hint of citrus, camphoric, or balsamic depending on the subspecies of tree. The oil is extracted from resin of the Frankincense tree, which appears as a giant shrub topped with abundant slender leaves and occasionally, small white flowers. It grows in some of the world's harshest dessert conditions. When the tree's bark is pierced with a knife, a milky-white resin is exuded. The resin is harvested and steam distilled to produce the pale yellow-green oil. Frankincense reduces both anxiety and stress and blends well with a wide variety of the calming oils.

Jasmine. A fragile evergreen, Jasmine is a climbing shrub that has dark green leaves and small, white star-shaped flowers. The flowers are usually harvested at night, when the aroma is most intense. Jasmine essential oil has a sweet, exotic, and richly floral smell. It is actually an absolute, extracted from the flowers of the jasmine plant using a solvent, rather than steam distillation. It takes a large number of jasmine blossoms to produce just a small volume of essential oil. Although expensive, this essential oil does more than just smell exquisite; it is known to lift depression and boost confidence and makes a wonderful additional to many calming blends.

Juniper. This essential oil is used to stimulate and strengthen the nerves and boost the spirit. It has a fresh, slightly woody aroma. Juniper is an evergreen shrub with blue-green needles and blue/black berries. The oil can be extracted from the dried berries, needles, and wood by steam distillation. The essential oil of the juniper berry is preferred to the oil distilled from the wood and needles so check for manufacture information carefully. Caution: Juniper oil should be diluted in a carrier oil, such as almond or grapeseed, due to its toxicity. Cautions: Avoid when pregnant or nursing or if you have any kidney/bladder issues.

Lavender. Probably one of the most popular oils for calming is lavender, which has a light fresh aroma. The lavender plant is an evergreen shrub with gray-green narrow leaves and beautiful purple/blue flowers. It is a hardy plant and can grow in almost any garden. Hence, there are many regional sources for this essential oil. The oil is extracted from the flowers of the plant, primarily through steam distillation. Lavender is an exception to the other oils. It does not need to be diluted in a carrier oil because it is so gentle. It has a very pleasant herbal and floral scent that balances mind and spirit. Caution: Lavender is one of the most commonly corrupted oils. If lavender essential oil is available at a very cheap price, chances are it is tainted or heavily diluted. It is also heavily associated with sleep so be careful when using it as a calming scent. It may work too well!

Lemongrass. A tradition in Indian medicine, lemongrass oil comes from a family of fragrant grasses, some of which grow to five feet. Lemongrass essential oil is extracted by steam distillation of the fresh or dried leaves of lemongrass. The oil is yellow in color with a citrus/lemon fragrance that is soft and clean. This unique oil has a strong balancing effect. It blends well with lavender, chamomile, clary sage, neroli and many of the citrus oils. Lemongrass is also a common flavor in Indonesian and Thai cooking and, like chamomile and bergamot, it is found in some teas.

Neroli. This is an exotic oil that is extracted from the white blossoms of the bitter orange tree. Neroli oil has a sweet, floral, and slightly citrus aroma and is pale yellow in color. It is also rather pricey since it requires a ton of orange blossoms to produce a quart of oil. The essential oil is extracted from the flowers by steam distillation. The oil's name is said to have originated from the Italian princess, Anne-Marie de la Tremoille (Countess of Nerola), who used the oil as a perfume and to scent her gloves. As with lavender, this is one of the most popular essential oils, as it not only has great therapeutic properties, but is considered one of the best aromatic stress relievers. It blends well with Ylang-ylang, jasmine, lavender, and the citrus oils.

Sandalwood. This oil from India creates a calming and harmonizing effect, while reducing tension and confusion. Sandalwood is an evergreen tree that burrows its roots into other trees. It can take thirty to sixty years for a tree to reach full maturity; thus, there are strict export regulations on India sandalwood. Sandalwood oil is extracted from the chipped heartwood by steam distillation. There are several sources of sandalwood and each has a unique odor. The scent is warm, balsamic, woodsy, and earthy. It has a euphoric yet grounding psychological effect that promotes a sense of well being.

Vanilla. A top calming essential oil is vanilla. Vanilla comes from an orchid native to Mexico. The vanilla plant is a flowering vine that produces long seeds pods. It is cultivated much like string beans, with a pole for support. The essential oil created from CO_2 extract has a rich, warm, and sweet scent. Not only is it one of the most pleasant fragrances of the oils, but it is an excellent stress reliever. It is a frequent scent in fragrance candles and lotions. It is also another scent that can be easily added to food from coffee to oatmeal or almond cookies. Caution: The oil is often artificially manufactured. Read labels carefully.

Vetiver. This essential oil has a wonderful effect on the mind and body and is useful to dispel irritability, anger, and hysteria. The plant is a tall, tufted perennial with long narrow leaves and an abundant complex lacework of underground white roots. It is mainly cultivated in the tropics and the oil is extracted from the roots by solvent extraction or steam distillation. The oil has an earthy, musty smell, much like the smell of a damp forest floor, and comes in a variety of colors. Vetiver oil is frequently used during meditation or prayer sessions due to its strong grounding quality. It is excellent for blending with neroli or one of the citrus oils.

Ylang-ylang. An essential oil that is similar to jasmine, ylang-ylang (pronounced as eee-lang, eee-lang) comes from a tall tropical tree about sixty feet high with large flowers. Native to Madagascar, the flower's scent is sweet, exotic, and sensual. A pale yellow color, ylang-ylang oil is extracted from the freshly picked flowers by several distillations. It is extremely helpful in dispelling stress, anxiety, and anger. It is a strong fragrance and can be blended with any of the calming oils.

Concentrate all your thoughts upon the work at hand.
The sun's rays do not burn until brought into focus.
~Alexander Graham Bell

Energizing Scents

Energizing scents are a quick way to perk up your mind. Some scents provide a boost of energy that improves performance and mood. Many of these scents work well together so be creative and explore different combinations.

Balsam pine. One of several evergreen scents, balsam pine oil conjures memories of Christmas for many since the Fir tree is the most common tree used during the holiday. The oil is steam distilled from the needles of the tree. The aroma of this clear oil is energizing but grounding. It blends well with other evergreen oils such as spruce, and cedarwood. A multi-evergreen mix can create a wonderful, complex deep forest aroma.

Basil. This essential oil has a fresh, sweet and slightly spicy aroma. Basil is a complex odor that is beneficial in fighting mental fatigue and can help stimulate/sharpen your sense of smell. In traditional Chinese medicine, basil is considered a cooling food. The essential oil is steam distilled from the whole flowering herb and the chemical composition varies greatly between plant varieties and growing locations. It blends well with clary sage, cypress, ginger, jasmine, rosemary, thyme, and several of the citrus oils. It is a dominating scent, however, so use lightly.

Cinnamon. A warming food in traditional Chinese medicine, cinnamon is a common spice used in cooking and baking. When looking to use in aromatherapy, many people use ground cinnamon or cinnamon sticks. Cinnamon increases brain activity, improves memory, and reduces nervousness. It can also be obtained in an essential oil. The oil can be steam distilled from either leaves or the bark of the tree. Although preferred, the bark oil does cause allergic reactions in some people and should be used well diluted. Caution: Cinnamon oil should not be used in a topical application.

Cypress. The oil is distilled from the fresh, dark green needles of a tall evergreen tree, which can grow to over 100 feet. The Cypress tree has slender branches and a statuesque conical shape, with small flowers and round cones. The principal action of Cypress oil is to enliven and regulate the flow of blood. Part of this action depends upon its restorative, toning effect on the veins, which is a by-product of its overall astringent quality. It may also increase concentration Cypress is an evergreen scent that mixes well with rose or juniper.

Ginger. The pale yellow oil from the ginger plant's root has a fresh woody-spicy aroma. It is gently stimulating and can enhance physical energy and courage. In traditional Chinese medicine, ginger is a warm herb with an affinity for the lungs and the intestines. It has a long history of healing and is often used to alleviate motion sickness. Ginger tea – either hot or cold - is an excellent pick-me-up! The oil is obtained from the root using a CO_2 extraction method. It blends well with lemongrass and the citrus oils.

Grapefruit. This essential oil is yellow and has a fresh, sweet citrus aroma. It is a strong energizing scent that also refreshes, cools, and cleanses. Grapefruit is considered a cooling food in Chinese medicine. Add grapefruit to a fruit or garden salad or drink grapefruit juice as a late-afternoon energy enhancer at a trial. The pleasing aroma has also been proven to have an appetite-reducing effect! Grapefruit essential oil is cold-pressed from the rind of ripe grapefruit. It blends well with frankincense, cedarwood, rosemary and the other citrus oils.

Lemon. One of the most common energizing essential oils, lemon has a refreshing, tangy-fruit aroma and is considered a cooling food in Chinese medicine. The oil is obtained through cold expression of the outer part of the fresh lemon peel. It can take up to three thousand lemons to produce a kilo of oil. Its gentle, calming effect promotes mental clarity and generally increases physical energy. Lemon oil contains limonene, which is responsible for the oil's citrus aroma, and citral, which is responsible for the lemony note. Caution: Lemon oil may make skin to which it is applied more sensitive to sunlight. Lemon oil blends well with a wide variety of the essential oils.

Orange. There are a variety of orange oils used in aromatherapy. Although they possess similar properties, orange oils are extracted from different parts of the orange tree. Sweet orange oil is cold-pressed produced from the fruit of the orange tree, while orange blossom is solvent extracted from the blossoms. Oranges are considered cooling foods in traditional Chinese medicine and they can provide an excellent emotional lift when eaten fresh. Orange oil has a fresh, tangy smell and it is frequently combined with other citrus and floral oils. Caution: Orange oil can make skin more sensitive to sunlight.

Peppermint. Mint has been used for thousands of years for its beneficial effects. As an essential oil, peppermint is considered indispensible by aromatherapists. The oil is steam distilled from the partially dried tops of the plants just before the herb begins to flower. The main constituent in peppermint is menthol which produces a cooling sensation and it is considered a cooling food in Chinese medicine. The aroma is fresh and sharp. The oil is strengthening, soothing, and stimulating and it can improve concentration and focus. Some peppermint oils are also food grade and can be added to your favorite recipes.

Rosemary. The aroma of this essential oil is warm and invigorating and it is considered to be a warm herb in traditional Chinese medicine. It strengthens mental awareness. Rosemary essential oil is steam distilled from whole rosemary herb, which is an evergreen brush with green-gray needles. It is pleasant addition to many aromatherapy formulas, particularly where the aroma is intended to stimulate the mind and get you moving

Thyme. The thyme plant is a perennial, evergreen herb with highly aromatic leaves. It gets its name from the Greek word *thymos* which means *to perfume.* There are two varieties of thyme essential oil used in aromatherapy: sweet thyme and red thyme. Each thyme oil has different properties and uses but the most common is sweet thyme. Thyme essential oil is water or steam distilled from the partially dried flowers or leaves of the plant. Red thyme is the crude distillate of the distillation process while sweet thyme is the second distillation of the herb. Sweet thyme essential oil has a sharp, woody aroma and is yellow in color. Its benefits include improved concentration, mental focus, and it helps overcome fatigue and exhaustion.

Excellence is not a skill. It is an attitude.
~Ralph Marston

Usage of Aromatherapy

As with all the calming tools and skills, you must practice at home before applying aromatherapy at a competitive event. There are three steps to the introduction of aromatherapy. First, go to a high-end drugstore or health food store and sniff your way through the essential oils. Select a few from each category: calming and energizing. This is an extremely individualized process. You can shop with a friend or partner but make your own selections! Second, test the scents you selected around your dog. Most essential oils have natural powers to sooth or to energize and many work on both humans and canines. Remember your olfactory system is directly linked to your emotional memory system and this applies to your dog also. What relaxes you, may actually stress your canine partner. Be sure to test each mix that you create or buy on your dog also. And, finally, you must determine which scents relax or energize you.

Take a three-day period and actively pay attention to your energy as you go through your day. Find the times in your daily routine where scent therapy can alter your mood for the better. For example, an energizing scent used after lunch can boost your mood for a more productive afternoon. An energy-scent left in your car can provide a tremendous pick-up as you drive home from work. A calming scent used before bed can ease you to sleep. I actually keep two small bottles of hand lotion in my backpack: one for stress relief and one for energy. Depending on the traffic and length of my drive, I can get a quick calm down or pick me up!

Scent application is not an exact science. Since each scent triggers both memory and mood, be conscious of which scents you use and how. For example, using a lavender lotion at bedtime can help you get to sleep. It can then be a tremendous sleep aid when traveling. Lavender will trigger your body for sleep which is wonderful when you are in a strange bed. However, if you then use lavender at a trial to calm down, you may pitch your energy-level right down to sleepy! Not a good plan when you need to memorize an advanced rally course!

In competition, you can use aromatherapy two ways: reactive and preemptive.

If an event or score or personal encounter with another competitor throws you out of balance, you can immediately apply aromatherapy to rebalance. As trainers we work constantly to balance our dog's energy to just the right level before entering the ring but we seldom manage our own. Aromatherapy gives you wonderful tool to maintain your energy level for a top-dog performance!

Alternately, you can plan when to use aromatherapy throughout your trial day or during an intense training session. Think through your last major competitive event. Analyze when you got tense, tired, or overly excited. You might get nervous just before you go in the ring or it might be during the warm-up. Perhaps you get shaky knees and a dry mouth just at the thought of training for a regional or National competition. On the other hand, after an early morning and the normal stress of the morning's competition, many people run out of pizzazz mid-afternoon. In all of these situations, your energy and emotions need a bit of adjustment. This is where you plan for scent therapy.

Even with just a few favorite scents to start with, there are easy ways to use aromatherapy at trials and at home.

Trial days. There are many ways to incorporate aromatherapy into your competition days.

• Keep your calming hand lotion in your training bag or video camera bag. Use the lotion before you begin your warm-up to soothe nerves and anxiety.

• Place a dot of essential oil on your wrists before you do your 4-7-8 breathing exercise. This works well if you feel jittery at the onset of your warm-up routine. With a dot of oil on your wrist, you can also take a source of calm with your right to the ring gate and even into the ring. In obedience, a subtle pass of your wrist or hand past your nose during a deep breath can calm any remaining nerves and settle your mind for the first exercise. Several of the advanced obedience exercises take time for the ring crew to setup. This is an excellent spot to work your breathing and use aromatherapy!

• Take along an essential oil or lotion that contains a good pick-me-up scent for use after lunch.

• Place a sachet in your car for an energy boost before the drive home. In order to keep scents fresh, place the sachet in a sealed plastic container. Storing the sachets also lets you alternate scents: calming for the drive to the competition and energizing on the way home!

• Bring a few extra sachets for the hotel room also. A familiar calming scent can make the room feel like home which calms both your nerves and your dogs. Another use for hotel rooms is to place a small sachet (or spray) of a high-level calming scent under your pillow. It can ease you into sleep in a strange location.

Scented bath salts. Mix twenty drops of your favorite essential oil with one tablespoon of a moisturizing carrier oil and three cups of Epsom salt. Common, easy to find carrier oils are extra virgin olive, sesame or sweet almond oil. Use half to one cup of bath salt per bath. Store bath salts in a sealed container. You can also purchase scented bath salts, like Dr Teal's which is available in a lavender, eucalyptus/spearmint or chamomile base.

Massage oil. Mix ten drops of essential oil or blend with one ounce of a carrier oil. Always be sure to test essential and carrier oils for skin sensitivity before using any product directly on your skin. Essential oils and blends should always be stored in air-tight dark glass containers. Again, like bath salts, if you do not want to mix your own, there are lots of pre-blended massage oils available on the internet or through specialty retailers.

Travel sachets. Gather the type of scents you would like to place in your sachet bag. Cinnamon sticks can be found in all grocery stores. Dried plants and flowers, like pine, rose, sage and lavender, can be found in specialty stores or spa boutiques. Sachet bags can be found in craft and retail stores.

Fill each sachet with dried flowers, plants or pieces of cinnamon stick. For combination scents and to enhance dried plant scent, you can add 1 or 2 drops of your favorite essential oils to the sachet to intensify the odor. For example, adding eucalyptus oil to lavender can give it an invigorating scent. Vanilla mixes well with cinnamon. Orange and ginger are another popular mix. Tie each bag with ribbon or a small rubber band. Be sure to fasten sachet bag tightly. Some sachet bags come with a drawstring, which makes it easier to seal the bag.

Place the sachet in an air tight container for use in your car and hotel rooms.

Stress relief ball. Create your own stress relief ball. These squishy balls can be purchased at almost any sporting goods store or from a physical therapist, but we have a simple, convenient way to make your own. Furthermore, we combine the stress relief of the squeeze and release with simple aromatherapy.

In order to make a stress relief ball, you will need:
* two medium balloons
* 1/3 cup dried rice
* 4-6 drops of one or two essential oils

Cut the stems off the two balloons. Use a spoon to stretch the top of one balloon and fill with dried rice. Once it's packed with rice, add in a few drops of your essential oil or blend of oils, then stretch the second balloon over the open hole of the filled balloon. If you want a super sturdy squishy ball, you can cover with a third balloon.

Home use. Put your favorite blend on a cotton ball in your vacuum bag or canister. The scent will be distributed through the air flowing through the vacuum

In order to succeed, we must
first believe that we can.
~ Nikos Kazantzakis

Music

Music has amazing power. It can reduce pain, enhance the immune system, reduce stress levels, retrain the brain after a traumatic injury, and even help your brain experience life differently. It can increase or decrease breathing rate and it can increase or decrease your heart rate. And, as you are now aware, with each physical response to music, there is a corresponding change in your conscious mind.

It is one of the easiest mind-body links to form and use. Furthermore, music can be used to calm or energize. A slow song can calm your mind while an upbeat, high tempo song can stimulate it. You may already be using music in your daily life to change your mood. Many people use music in the car as an energizer or relaxer. Runners workout with an I-pod and gym rats play music during workouts to distract their mind from tedium and many use upbeat music during difficult sets to push harder.

Music is not just for car travel, gym workouts, or sleep routines. For competing athletes, music provides a direct pathway from body to mind. Think about how often your body goes into motion – bouncing knees, tapping fingers, bopping head, moving feet – when you hear an upbeat song. It doesn't really matter what your mental state was before the song. When your body goes into motion, your mind just follows. And, if you have a strong, positive emotional response to the song your mood can be almost euphoric within seconds! Alternately, a few slow songs can induce yawns, drooping eyes, and steady deep breathing. The slow beat of the music slows your entire body down.

Music Motivation

Kathleen and I sometimes use music to energize a late evening class, particularly in the winter when it's been dark for several hours. The students frequently arrive with a low energy level. We crank up the I-Pod boombox with a set of upbeat songs. The music re-energizes the students, gets them moving thru the first walk-thru with a bounce (and the occasional dance step), and makes the whole class a lot more fun.

Music Selection

Choosing music is an intensely personal choice. A song that you find calming may drive your training partner absolutely batty. Kathleen and I have this problem in the car! My idea of upbeat music seems slow and boring to her while some of her rap music rattles my nervous system. Thankfully, with I-pod playlists and satellite radio, we have enough choices to comprise.

As individuals, everyone will have favorites to listen to while jogging, driving, working, training or competing at trials. You must make your own music selections.

Some points to consider when selecting music....

Tempo is important. Upbeat music has between 120-140 beats per minute, which also happens to be the standard tempo for dance music. This is also the range that scientists have found to be immune enhancing. Fast tempo music is useful for workouts and high energy times, such as during an afternoon walk-thru at an agility trial. Medium or slow tempo music is a good choice when you are nervous or need to relax completely, like right be going to sleep. When you create playlists, keep music with like tempos grouped together.

Music can change the world because it can change people
~Bono

Rhythm is both felt and heard. Your body has its own physical rhythm, most notably your heart rate and breathing patterns, but it also has a physical response to the rhythm of any given piece of music. Many scientists believe that your response (like or dislike) to a song is dependent on its tempo being close to your body's physical state when you hear it. For example, if you are relaxed or almost asleep, then a high-tempo musical piece may be irritating. Alternately, that same piece of music, heard while you are working on a project or cleaning the house, can be effective and stimulating. During a workout, I frequently listen to very high tempo music that I find extremely irritating at any other time during the day.

When selecting songs, pay attention to which ones make you want to get up and boogie, bop, or rock around the room. These are the songs that will create energy when you hear them later. The opposite is then also true. If the song encourages you to breathe deeply and loosens tension in your jaw, shoulders, or neck, then you have a good song to add to the relaxing playlist.

Music is a strong mental anchor. Music is easy for your mind to associate with past events and/or people. Mental anchors are memories linked closely to smells, sounds, or emotional situations. Be on guard for songs that are anchored to sad or disappointing memories. On the flip side, you may find music linked to happy memories or successful situations to have an incredibly strong impact on your mood.

Visual messages should match music. Songs that have a music video, are used in a movie sound track, are incorporated into a TV show, or are linked to a specific YouTube video often have strong visual messages attached to them. The music might have the correct tempt, have great lyrics, and be easy to sing but the remembered visual message may not positively affect your mood. The visual images of the screen may overwrite the impact of the song. Beware of your mind's underlying association.

On the flip side, using songs from movies like Secretariat (*It's Who You Are*), Rocky III (*Eye of the Tiger*), Chariots of Fine (theme song), or The Lion King (*Circle of Life*), carry strong messages of survival and success. And, when choosing music, remember your association may be different than a friend or training partner's.

For competitive athletes, music provides a direct pathway from body to mind no matter where you are competing. The right song can send you into a deep sleep or send you dancing across the floor!

Listen carefully to the lyrics within a song. Although the music may be upbeat and the rhythm might work, if the words within the song are depressing, discouraging, or upsetting, then the overall affect of the music on your mood will be negative. This is very important with regards to today's current pop songs. There are always hidden meanings and attitudes within a song. Be sure you know what the song is about before you add it to your playlist. On the other hand, the lyrics, like those from Hall of Fame by Daniel O'donoghue, James Barry, Will Adams, and Mark Sheehan, are excellent for a pre-performance lift!

Hall of Fame

Yeah, you can be the greatest
You can be the best
You can be the King Kong banging on your chest
You could beat the world
You could beat the war
You could talk to God, go banging on his door
You can throw your hands up
You can beat the clock (yeah)
You can move a mountain
You can break rocks
You can be a master
Don't wait for luck

Dedicate yourself and you gon' find yourself
Standing in the hall of fame (yeah)
And the world's gonna know your name (yeah)
'Cause you burn with the brightest flame (yeah)
And the world's gonna know your name (yeah)
And you'll be on the walls of the hall of fame

You can go the distance
You can run the mile
You can walk straight through hell with a smile
You could be the hero
You could get the gold
Breaking all the records they thought never could be broke
Yeah, do it for your people
Do it for your pride
How you ever gonna know if you never even try?
Do it for your country
Do it for your name
'Cause there's gonna be a day

When you're standing in the hall of fame (yeah)
And the world's gonna know your name (yeah)
'Cause you burn with the brightest flame (yeah)
And the world's gonna know your name (yeah)
And you'll be on the walls of the hall of fame

Be a champion, be a champion, be a champion, be a champion
On the walls of the hall of fame

Music Use

In order to incorporate music into your quest to link body and mind, you need to have music readily available. Since you must be able to play the right type of song to correctly alter your mood, if you haven't already, you need to invest in twenty-first century technology. Think Apple.

1 - Purchase an I-Pod. It does not have to be an expensive one. The I-Pod Nano has more than enough memory. If you are unsure about what technology to purchase, how to buy songs, etc....find a teenager and take them shopping! The X-generation was born with an I-pod gene!

2 - Load up the music and then divide your songs into playlists corresponding to the moods you are trying to achieve. Create different, small playlists for mood control. Create a playlist for relaxation, a playlist for motivation, and a playlist for sleep. In order to keep the music fresh, you can create multiple playlists under each category. Twenty songs are more than enough for a playlist.

3 - Maintain your song playlists. Make it a habit to add music monthly (at least). Think of your satellite radio as a huge shopping network for music! You should also be diligent about removing music that is no longer interesting, becomes boring, or develops a negative association thru an event or some visual image.

Food and Nutrition

We all know about waist-line nutrition. You can pick a low-fat, no-fat, high-fat, low-carb, high-carb, liquid, vegetable, cookie, or organic diet and count calories, fat, carbs, or points on your quest to lose weight. Some of these diets have been around for decades and new ones appear daily on the Internet and in bookstores. Thankfully, the traditional focus of a diet is slowly changing from weight-loss to proper nutrition, which is quite likely more important than calorie and fat counting. There are also plenty of diets tailored for bulk or lean muscle building and diets tailored to ease health problems, such as heart disease, high cholesterol, or diabetes. Regardless of whether you are a naturally nutritional-savvy eater or are working on a diet for weight-loss or a health benefit, you need to look at the fine print beneath your diet.

It is very true…you are what you eat!

Diets tailored for high-performance athletes are available almost anywhere but are mostly designed for body builders, runners, or other high-intensity sports. Dog events are athletic events with two highly trained athletes. And yet, a Google search on "dog agility diets" returns only a fraction of the hits when compared to "golf diets" or even "archery diets." And, of course, the diet information returned by the Google search engine is for the dog!

Diet and nutrition are huge components of an optimal performance. Consider how many hours you've spent in the past discussing the pros and cons of a raw vs kibble diet for your dog. How many dog food bag labels have you read? Most high-level competitors can easily tell you the protein and fat content of their dogs' food but have no idea how much protein or fat is in an egg, a yogurt, or a hamburger!

Dietary habits significantly affect your body weight, body composition, and physical health. They also impact your strength, stamina, and mental focus. All of us are well aware of the basics of a healthy diet. As athletes, however, we need to consider more than just calorie intake and fat content. Muscle recovery, joint health, and brain nutrition should also be part of every nutrition decision.

A few of the popular sports diets can be tailored for canine sports competitors. However, each canine event offers its own challenges. The mental concentration required for a five minute utility test is very similar to riding a dressage test or to shooting in an archery match. Most agility courses require the human to be as agile as a tennis player and have the speed of a sprinter and often on a less than desirable surface! Disc dog competitors need much of the same coordination, timing, and strength of a gymnast or football wide receiver. So what does your body need to fuel it through an intense one-hour obedience practice or a twelve-hour day containing five agility runs?

Basically, your body is a chemical warfare site. All day, every day your systems, like digestive, circulatory, endocrine, nervous, immune and several others, are in a constant state of flux. There is no constant state for any of the systems that integrate to make you. A machine can be on or off. Living organisms are always on. Furthermore, physical and mental activities add additional demands to your systems creating large functional swings, such as the release of large amounts of insulin after a high dose of sugar or release of the hormone cortisol in response to stress. It is these out-of-balance conditions that a well balanced diet attempts to aid. With conscious attention to the demands you are placing on your body and mind, you can smooth out the greater peaks and valleys that occur during a sporting event. The goal is to nourish the entire body. High fiber, complex carbohydrates keep your blood sugar level even. Proteins provide the raw material to create the amino acids needed

Food is an important part of a balanced diet.
~Fran Libowitz

by biochemical processes throughout the body and consuming unsaturated fats provides the correct levels of essential fatty acids.

You do not need to become a registered nutritionist or read every label in the grocery store. A little bit of knowledge goes a long way for athletes and a few minor changes can have a profound effect on your performances. Like the other tools for calming your mind, nutrition is a building block. It impacts how you feel and perform all day. Paying attention to which foods create energy and which induce calm is a huge start. Knowing which foods impact your body's health and recovery, your brain's nutrition, and your overall energy state is critical for a peak performance.

Brain Nutrition

One of the least considered aspects of most diets is brain health. Have you ever considered what nutrients are needed for a healthy brain? It is after all the most important organ in your body and determines how you function and feel!

Just like muscles, your brain needs to stay conditioned for a top-dog performance. What nutrients does your brain need to remain focused, calm and alert all day? Brain nutrition is critical and yet many people, even on a good day, have a brain that is malnourished or just getting by. Your brain needs vitamins, minerals and protein just like your body but in your brain a deficiency is often obvious in emotions and behavior. Fortunately, the brain responds almost immediately when provided the proper nutrition.

Food preparation and presentation is an art and is well covered by the Internet, bookstores, and cable television. This is not a cookbook or a diet plan. It is a guide to help you perform at your absolute best in every athletic situation. Understanding how your body and brain use food for fuel is a critical skill for successful competitors. Dieting is a beat-up topic but this is not about calories or fat. This is about eating well so you can function at your best with a body and brain primed for maximum effort. With this information, you are reaching your brain thru your stomach.

Just as it is for your canine partner, your energy, mood and mental focus are by-products of dietary intake. Taking a smart brain and a body infused with energy into every training session and competition requires a sound nutrition plan that balances proteins with fats, carbohydrates, minerals, vitamins and roughage (fiber). You do not need to be a dietician but taking time to learn the basics will provide you with another control point for your thoughts and emotions. With a well nourished

The brain is only about 2% of a person's body mass but requires about 20% of its oxygen and calories.

brain, positive thinking is natural, time management is effortless, and routines are smoothly adhered to.

Protein. Protein is broken down in the body into amino acids. The amino acids – eight of which are considered essential because your body cannot synthesize them – are then used to assemble the thousands of different proteins the human body needs to function. Dietary proteins fall into two groups – complete and incomplete. Complete proteins contain ample amounts of all eight essential amino acids. Fish, meat, eggs, cheese, and yogurt are complete proteins. Grains, legumes, seeds, nuts, and a variety of other foods are incomplete proteins, because they only provide some of the essential amino acids. Proteins are especially important for brain nutrition. In the brain, amino acids are used to build neurotransmitters, including acetylcholine, norepinephrine, serotonin, and dopamine. Neurotransmitters are used by neurons to "talk."

Fats. Our brains need fat. Brain health is dependent on a consistent source of good fat (monounsaturated). New evidence and studies are suggesting that monounsaturated fats maintain and enhance memory and learning and prevent diseases. Conversely, the same studies are showing that bad fats (saturated and artificial trans fats) reduce brain functions and memory.

A fat is designated as saturated or unsaturated based on the proportion of fatty acids present. (All fats contain both saturated and unsaturated fatty acids.) Saturated fats are generally solid at room temperature and tend to be from animal products, think cheese and butter. Unsaturated fats are often liquid at room temperature and are usually plant-based, like olive oil, sesame seeds, avocado, or walnuts.

There are also two types of unsaturated fat that your body and brain need: omega-3 and omega-6. These are essential because our bodies cannot synthesize them. Food sources of omega-3 are fish, shellfish, flaxseed, walnuts, and green leafy vegetables. Omega-6 or linoleic acid is common in American diets. It comes primarily from corn, soy, sesame oil, eggs, sunflower seeds, walnuts, and pumpkin seeds. TCM seeks to balance omega-3 and -6 fats.

Carbohydrates. There are two types of carbohydrates: complex and simple sugars. Your digestive system converts both types of carbohydrates into glucose, a form of sugar carried in the blood and transported to cells for energy. Simple sugars are converted very easily and quickly into glucose. Complex carbohydrates are converted slower; thus providing your body with a steadier supply of glucose over a longer time period. Your brain uses glucose for fuel. Without an adequate supply of glucose, your body enters ketosis, a metabolic state in which the body uses ketones for energy. This can interfere with brain function and can reduce energy levels. There is also some evidence that a low-carbohydrate diet leads to negative moods.

While competing or training hard, your brain needs food. A consistent supply of glucose is necessary but it does not need to be from simple sugars. A much better source of glucose is from complex carbohydrates, like whole grains, potatoes, beans, rice, fruit, and vegetables. Furthermore, glucose not used by the cells is converted into glycogen - another form of carbohydrate that is stored in the muscles and liver. After training or competing, an athlete's body has depleted its stores of

> *As athletes, we need to consider more than just calorie intake and fat content. Muscle recovery, joint health, and brain nutrition should also be part of every nutrition decision.*

glycogen. Replenishing glycogen stores is especially important for athletes who compete multiple times in a day.

Minerals. These are inorganic elements that occur in the body and are required to support biochemical processes. Some of the more important minerals are potassium, sodium, calcium, phosphorus, magnesium, iron, and chloride. Other trace elements needed by the human body are zinc, iron, manganese, copper, iodine, selenium and molybdenum. Magnesium in particular is an important brain nutrient.

Vitamins. A vitamin is any organic compound required by the body, even in small amounts. There are thirteen essential vitamins, which are classified according to their ability to be absorbed in fat or water. The fat-soluble vitamins include vitamin A, vitamin D, vitamin E, and vitamin K. Only vitamin D can be manufactured by the body. Water-soluble vitamins include the eight B vitamins and vitamin C.

There are eight B vitamins, which are frequently listed on nutrition labels by their name.

> B1 is thiamine.
> B2 is riboflavin.
> B3 is niacin.
> B5 is pantothenic acid.
> B6 is pyroxidine.
> B7 is biotin (sometimes referred to as vitamin H).
> B9 is folic acid.
> B12 is cobalamin.

Vitamin C is also known as ascorbic acid. Vitamin C and the Bs cannot be stored by the body so they must be consumed frequently. They need to be ingested daily since they are critical vitamins for optimum athletic performance. Vitamin E and C function as antioxidants and the brain is particularly sensitive to damage by free radicals. Many of the B vitamins are especially important for high-level brain functions since they are used in the formation of brain chemicals like dopamine, epinephrine, and serotonin.

Fiber. Fiber is a type of carbohydrate that the human body cannot digest. It is necessary for correct digestion and absorption of the minerals and vitamins you eat.

Your diet is a bank account.
Good food choices are good investments.
~ Bethenny Frankel

Nutrition for Competition

Eating for taste is fun. Eating for nutrition is smarter and an absolute must for athletes who want to maximize their potential. Knowing how your body processes the different types of foods and which foods work to change your energy level and mental focus can make a tremendous difference in your performance.

An easy starting point for analyzing your diet as an athlete is to examine your intake levels of water, caffeine, alcohol, and foods that contain refined carbohydrates. Water is an absolute must - regardless of temperature – and always has a positive influence. Foods that contain vitamins, minerals, and proteins make good choices for competition days. Many of these can actually alter your mood and help manage your emotions. Adequate protein intake can stabilize your energy level throughout the day. On the other hand, caffeine, alcohol, and refined carbohydrates can wreck havoc with your blood sugar levels, leaving you tired and unfocused during competition.

A few simple food choices will make a big difference in your ability to manage your mind and keep your body moving well. The following items are just for your consideration and knowledge. They are not intended to be diet rules.

Water. Sixty percent of the human body is water. Seventy percent of the brain is water. Your lungs are close to ninety percent water. And, blood is around eighty percent water. Each day humans need to replace about 2.4 liters (85 ounces) of water. Think five bottles of water. If adults should drink eighty-five ounces of water a day, then athletes should drink much more.

I pay attention to my diet to be a healthier gymnast but I'm not obsessive over it.
~ Shawn Johnson

Before you panic about all that water consumption, remember that many foods and beverages contain water. Not all water must be consumed as water! For example, a Snapple Green Tea is 17.5 ounces, a large coffee is typically 16 ounces and even milk has a high water content. Most fruits and vegetables contain up to ninety percent water. You don't need to walk around with a pocket calculator totaling up water ounces every day. The goal is to increase your awareness of how much water you are consuming and to keep it high.

Drink to think!

Train yourself to drink – water that is! Adequate hydration delays fatigue and keeps athletes performing well. Carry multiple water bottles to long practices and to trials. If the water bottle is in your hand, you will be much more likely to drink from it. Time and practice are required to increase your consumption of adequate water but awareness must come first.

Many athletes — even top-caliber athletes — routinely become slightly to severely dehydrated during training and competition. By the time you actually register being thirsty, you are already dehydrated! Sweat evaporation is the primary way of dissipating excess heat and you sweat mostly water. Without adequate water intake, sweating slows and thus cooling slows. Dehydration also impairs mental performance. The human body cannot adapt to dehydration. Decreased blood volume due to dehydration also reduces blood flow to the skin, which further impairs heat dissipation. Research indicates that a person who is as little as two percent dehydrated can experience up to a ten percent decline in performance, and it gets worse from there.

Bottom line…make a conscious effort to drink water regularly throughout the day and to drink small amounts frequently while working out or competing.

Caffeine. Caffeine is a stimulant. It increases the activity of your nervous system. Like many things in life, caffeine is fine when used in moderation. However, when you jazz up your system on caffeine, there are consequences. Some beverages are loaded with caffeine and you might be surprised by the amounts. Caffeine is only a problem when you consume too much or go over your own tolerance level.

Currently, caffeine is not listed on nutrition labels so you will need to do your own research. Know what you are ingesting! For your favorite beverage, check the product website or check websites that list caffeine content for the latest brands and information.

◆ *Coffee*. An 8-oz cup of brewed or drip coffee has about 100-150 mg of caffeine. A cup of instant coffee has roughly 50 mg. Your coffee shop coffees have considerably more caffeine. A Starbucks Grande coffee has a whopping 330 mg of caffeine. Cut down to the Tall and you are still ingesting 260 mg. A large Dunkin Donuts coffee has around 200 mg. Einstein Bros is closer to Starbucks with 300 mg in their large coffee. As a general rule, lattes and mochas have less caffeine than the regular coffees. Decaff coffee has anywhere from 3-12 mg of caffeine for each 8 oz.
Most of us stick to a favorite brand or company for our morning joe. On the road, however, you may buy your coffee from another store. This is where trailing away from home starts to get difficult. If you are a DD drinker and switch to Starbucks on the road, you are starting your morning with double the caffeine. Talk about jangled nerves! Alternately, if you are a Starbucks customer and can only find a Dunkin Donuts near your hotel, you are starting your morning with half the caffeine you are used to. Your fuzziness during the walk-thru now has an explanation!

◆ *Soda and energy drinks*. The bewildering variety of soda choices is easily matched by the surprising amount of caffeine in any given brand or variety. A can of Coke Classic has 35 mg while a Diet Coke has 45 mg. Mountain Dew – regular or diet - has 55 mg. A Diet Pepsi has 36 mg, Pepsi One has 55 mg, and a regular Pepsi has 38 mg. A can of diet or regular Dr Pepper or Sunkist Orange has about 40 mg of caffeine. Most root beers, despite the dark color, have very little or no caffeine. Even Crystal Light Energy has 120 mg while Focus has 40 mg. Energy drinks are obviously intentionally loaded with caffeine. They run anywhere from Jolt Energy at 280 mg to 5-Hour Energy at 200 mg to AMP at 72 mg. Even Vitamin Water – Energy has 40 mg of caffeine.

◆ *Tea*. There is less caffeine in tea. A brewed cup of regular tea has 45-50 mg of caffeine in 8 oz. Green tea has 20-25 mg. Black tea has more caffeine, anywhere from 40-120 mg. For tea, make your choice Green Tea. It contains an amino acid known as L-theanine, which has a calming effect on the brain by altering the levels of several neurotransmitters, resulting in a feeling of peace and calm. L-theanine may override the stimulant affect of the caffeine. Although some people who are extremely sensitive to caffeine may not get this response, most people report feel more relaxed when they drink a cup of green tea. What about the bottled ice teas? Arizona Green Tea has 15 mg in 16 oz, while Lipton Lemon has 7 mg in its 12 oz. A 20 oz Lipton Ice Tea has 50 mg, while a Nestea Ice Tea has 34 mg in 16 oz. For caffeine reduction, tea is a much healthier choice than either coffee or soda. Herbal teas contain no caffeine. A cup of Chamomile, Rosehips, or Lemon Verbena is wonderful for stress and anxiety reduction.

• *Other products*. Then there is chocolate. A 1.45 oz bar of Hershey's dark chocolate has 31 mg of caffeine. Several Ben and Jerry's coffee ice creams have 80+ mg of caffeine in an 8 oz serving. Be wary also of coffee-flavored yogurts. There is even caffeine in Excedrin…2 extra strength tablets have 130 mg of caffeine. If the Excedrin doesn't take care of your headache, you will be wide awake to suffer through it! Midol has similar levels of caffeine per tablet.

Looking good and feeling good go hand in hand. If you have a healthy lifestyle, your diet and nutrition are set, and you're working out, you are going to feel good.
~Jason Statham

Alcohol. Alcohol is a drug, but it is also a nutrient because it provides energy. It affects all cells in the body but the most immediate physiological and psychological effects are on the brain. Although classified as a depressant drug, alcohol frequently elicits a short-term stimulant effect. The affects and durations are dependent on your blood alcohol concentration, which is influenced by the amount of alcohol consumed for your body size, body fat content, and gender. Alcohol is metabolized extremely quickly by the body. Unlike foods, which require time for digestion, alcohol needs no digestion and about 20 percent is absorbed directly across the walls of an empty stomach. The first rush of alcohol can reach the brain within one minute. Although the short term affect of alcohol might be a relaxed, worry-free state, the longer term affects make it incompatible with most sporting activities. For athletes, one of the biggest problems with alcohol consumption is the ensuing dehydration. After a day outdoors, either in hot, cold, or windy weather, your body may already be slightly dehydrated, consuming alcohol simply makes it worse. For each alcoholic drink, drink a bottle of water to minimize its effects.

Refined carbohydrates. Your body was not intended to consume sweets and foods made from refined carbohydrates, also known as processed flour and sugar. Highly processed white flour (listed as enriched wheat flour or wheat flour) is made without the two most nutritious and fiber-rich parts of the wheat grain: the outside bran layer and the germ. Thus, wheat flour is converted almost immediately by your body into sugar and enters the bloodstream rapidly. Your pancreas, the organ that regulates how much insulin is released into the blood, is caught off guard by sudden surges of sugar. Sensing that it has more work to do than it really does, the pancreas releases too much  insulin. The result is chemical warfare! With too much insulin in your system, you then have a dramatic drop in blood sugar (usually within the hour). The result is a feeling of lethargy, mental confusion, weakness, and false feelings of hunger.

As the initial sugar rush wanes in response to the increased insulin, there is another consequence. The sudden blood sugar drop releases stress hormones! Before long, you will feel more jangled than before you inhaled that piece of chocolate-frosted MACH cake! Furthermore, many processed foods are made with saturated fats and large amounts of sodium and simple sugar. If the label lists sugar, sucrose, fructose, corn syrup, white or wheat flour, the food contains refined carbohydrates. If these are at the top of the ingredients list, the product contains mostly simple carbohydrates.

Common sources of refined carbohydrates are table sugar, fruit juice, corn syrup, pastas made from white flour, white bread made from wheat flour, cake, cookies, candy, breakfast cereals, and packaged snack foods, like chips, crackers, and cheese snacks. If you do shop for these foods, look for products that are made with whole grains, have high fiber, are low in sodium, and are free of saturated fats.

Smart Food Choices

All foods are not created equal. Some foods can make your nervous system a frenzied mess while others can usher you smoothly asleep. Many foods alter your mood by changing the proportions of neurotransmitter levels in your brain. Most athletes need a competition diet that raises serotonin levels, which helps reduce stress and anxiety. Raising serotonin levels can also lower the stress hormone cortisol. Other consumable stress-reducers are vitamins B, C, and E along with minerals like manganese, selenium and zinc.

All of the following are suggestions for trials, long practices sessions, and tournaments. Some make great meals and snacks to pack for the day. Others make excellent choices for dinner before and during tournaments and multi-day events. Everyone has different nutritional needs and stress points, where their energy needs

> *In traditional Chinese medicine, foods are not considered bad or good. They are just used inappropriately or appropriately.*

to be managed. The foods listed here are what Kathleen, I and our students have found useful. You may like these or you may find others that work better. The key is to create a system that manages your nutrition on critical days.

You do not have to eat all of them and can avoid what you don't like. You'll not find me munching on brussel sprouts anytime soon! However, I do pack and consume bananas, berries, oatmeal cookies, oranges, eggs, and turkey regularly at trials and during long training sessions. Kathleen prefers trail mixes, chicken wraps, and raw vegetables.

Asparagus. Each crispy stalk is a source of vitamin C and vitamin B9 (folic acid), a natural mood-lightener. Dip the spears in low-fat yogurt for a hit of calcium and vitamin D. I don't wander around agility trials munching asparagus stalks but I will choose or even ask for them at a restaurant and do put them on the home menu during trial weekends.

Avocados. If you're craving something creamy, look no further. Avocados are loaded with vitamins. They have vitamin A and C and B, particularly B1, B2, and B6. Your body quickly depletes B vitamins under stress and none of the B vitamins can be stored. So replenishing them is crucial to maintaining nerve and brain cell functions. Another plus, avocados creaminess comes from a healthy fat. In traditional Chinese medicine (TCM), it is considered a cooling food.

Bananas. A ripe, yellow banana is a good source of dietary fiber, vitamin C, potassium, manganese, and vitamin B6. Bananas are also an excellent source of potassium and melatonin. To handle stress, you need to maintain a correct balance between sodium and potassium. Acute stress increases adrenal gland activity, resulting in a rise in the secretion of the hormone aldosterone, which causes sodium to be retained in kidneys and subsequently the soft tissues. Sodium retention by aldosterone is part of the fight-flight reaction to stress. Limiting your salt intake and eating potassium rich foods like bananas can help your body recover faster after stress. It is not surprising that TCM considers bananas a cooling food!

Bananas do no need to be consumed as whole bananas. It is easy to incorporate homemade banana bread or banana cookies into your trial diet. Making them yourself lets you replace some sugar with honey and you can add yogurt, dried fruits, and nuts. After several years of tweaking, my banana bread recipe is made with yogurt and honey and includes dark chocolate, vanilla protein powder, and walnuts. It is filling and balancing for both breakfast and lunch!

Remember bananas also make a great snack for your canine partner!

Berries. Raspberries, blackberries, blueberries, cranberries, strawberries - any berry can satisfy your body's request for glucose without the sugar high. The carbohydrates in berries get turned into glucose very slowly. Thus, you won't have a blood sugar high and subsequent crash. For example, one cup of blackberries has 14g of carbohydrates but only 7 g of sugar and 8 g of dietary fiber. Blackberries are also very high in antioxidants and are an excellent source of vitamin C, which helps fight the stress hormone cortisol. Of all the berries, strawberries have the highest vitamin C content and are also a good source of potassium. Blueberries are an excellent source of antioxidants, are considered by many to be excellent brain food, and are great to share with your pup.

During winter months, when berries are harder to find and the cost can actually impact our trial budget, we switch to dried cherries, cranberries, blueberries and the old stand-by – raisins. Whole frozen fruit is also an excellent off-season choice and gets mixed well into yogurt or put on salads.

Blackstrap molasses. Unlike refined sugar and corn syrup, which are stripped of virtually all nutrients except simple carbohydrates, or artificial sweeteners, which provide no useful nutrients, blackstrap molasses is a healthy sweetener that contains a variety of minerals, is low in calories, and is fat free. In addition to providing quickly assimilated carbohydrates, blackstrap molasses can increase your energy by helping to replenish your iron stores. Blackstrap molasses is a very good source of iron, calcium, copper, manganese, potassium and magnesium. Check your grandma's cookbook or the web for a good molasses cookie recipe. Furthermore, many molasses cookie recipes call for ginger, which is an excellent natural herb that soothes the stomach. Most herbologists recommend ginger for motion sickness but the same principal applies the rolling-stomach nausea of waiting for your run-off for high-in-trial at the Obedience Invitational. So, bake a batch of molasses cookies and take a few along to your next trail.

Brussels sprouts. These green orbs are a great source of B vitamins and vitamin C. Both are useful vitamins when you are in a stressful situation. Again, not exactly a travel food, but you can include on the dinner menu.

The dog that trots about finds a bone.
~Golda Meir

Carrots. Carrots are a goldmine of nutrients. No other vegetable or fruit contains as much carotene as carrots, which the body converts to vitamin A. This is a truly versatile vegetable and an excellent source of vitamins B and C. Raw carrots are also about 87% water and contain vitamin C, vitamin B6, B1, B9, magnesium and potassium. Like bananas, carrots are made for traveling. You can eat whole, sliced or julienne (with or without dip) and get a dose of water, fiber and vitamins at any time or anywhere. Chomping on carrots is also a great stress reducer!

Grains (complex carbohydrates). Whole grains, such as barley, buckwheat, oats, and rice, contain complex carbohydrates. Every cell in your body uses carbohydrates for energy, particularly your brain. With the popularity of low-carb diets, many people are afraid to eat carbohydrates and do not distinguish between the health-robbing effects of simple sugars and refined carbohydrates and the health-giving properties of complex carbohydrates. Consuming complex carbohydrates is particularly important for athletes, whose bodies need a constant source of energy. Complex carbohydrates are high-fiber foods, including grains, fruits, and vegetables. They help stabilize the blood sugar, which keeps your energy at an even level.

Sources of Tryptophan

Many whole grains, nuts (sesame seeds, peanuts, dried sunflower seeds, cashews, walnuts, dried pumpkin seeds), fish and turkey are natural sources of tryptophan. A steady supply of tryptophan can increase levels of serotonin in the brain, producing a calming effect. Whole grains and nuts also keep insulin levels stable and a steady insulin release may make it easier for tryptophan to nudge itself into the brain. Keeping tryptophan levels at an optimum level is easy if you swap refined carbohydrates for whole grains - think whole-grain bread rather than white for your sandwich - or munch on a small bag of nuts for your mid-afternoon snack.

Dark chocolate. Dark chocolate is simply chocolate that contains more cocoa than regular or milk chocolate. Select a chocolate that contains at least fifty percent cocoa. Dark chocolate contains the neurotransmitter anandamide, which resembles THC, a chemical found in marijuana. In the brain, both THC and anadamide activate the same receptor, which raises dopamine levels. A higher dopamine level generally leads to a feeling of well being. Unlike THC, anadamide is found naturally in the 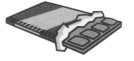 brain so it breaks down very rapidly. Chocolate, however, contains two other chemicals that work to slow the breakdown of the anandamide; thus extending the feelings of well-being. Dark chocolate is also a source of other biochemicals that may play a role in altering mood: phenylethylamine and theobromine. Phenylethylamine, known as the chocolate amphetamine, causes changes in blood pressure and blood-sugar levels, which produce feelings of excitement and alertness. Theobromine can help with mental and physical relaxation and can act as a stimulant, similar to caffeine.

Dark chocolate is also rich in tryptophan and has antioxidants, called flavonoids. The flavonoids in chocolate seem to be more biologically active and thus more useful to the body. Of course, all the good comes at a cost. Dark chocolate has a high fat content. Fortunately, the fat in chocolate is mostly a saturated vegetable fat, like olive and canola oils.

Both Kathleen and I are partial to dark chocolate covered almonds and walnuts. Combining the two makes an excellent snack food at trials or during long training sessions.

Eggs. The little white egg is an excellent source of protein and nutrients. A medium egg is high in vitamin A, vitamin B2 and B12. Although high in fat, the majority of the fat is unsaturated. An egg salad sandwich on whole grain bread is an excellent choice for lunch and hard-boiled eggs travel well. Take along an extra to share with your dog as a mid-day snack.

Fish. Tuna, salmon, flounder, catfish, haddock, trout....fish is a superb source of protein. A serving of fish contains healthy fats, which reduce your cholesterol, and omega-3 fatty acids, which help keep your heart healthy and can improve your mood. Many of the fishes also support good brain health. Fish is well known as diet choice of many healthy contrarians around the world and it is a neutral TCM food. Salmon and mackerel have the highest omega-3 contents. Salmon is also an excellent source of vitamin D, B12, B6 and magnesium. All fish are not the same. Nutrition content varies by species and how and where the fish were raised. Check carefully for the source of the fish. Fish that is farm raised is not the same as wild caught (there are pros and cons to both) and imported fish may contain toxins not found in fish raised in the United States or wild caught.

A tuna fish sandwich on a whole grain bagel or bread is a good lunch food. Another excellent way to add fish is to make it your standard selection when eating out. Grilled salmon or tuna for dinner is an awesome choice when trialing on the road.

Honey. In his book, *Alkalize or Die*, Dr. Theodore Baroody discusses how eating raw, organic honey can help people calm down and fall asleep more easily. Raw honey is predigested in bees before it reaches our tables, so it's easy to digest and packed with nutrients. It's high in potassium, which neutralizes acids in the body, and assists naturally occurring tryptophan to relax the body. Use honey in all your recipes as a sugar substitute.

Kiwifruit. This green fruit is an excellent source of vitamin C and a very good source of dietary fiber. It is also a good source of the minerals potassium, magnesium and copper, and is a good source of the antioxidant vitamin E. Kiwi is a cooling food in TCM and makes an excellent addition to fruit salads or smoothies.

Begin to be now what you will be hereafter.
~William James

Milk. Milk contains the naturally occurring amino acid known as tryptophan, which is used by the brain to create serotonin. Obviously, milk is also high in calcium, which assists the body in the processing of tryptophan. On the flip side, milk gets a bad rap for having too many residual chemicals and/or hormones. It is worth noting that TCM eliminates milk and other dairy products or uses in moderation. As a general rule, TCM considers a high dairy diet to be unbalancing. As a consumer of foods versus a nutritionist or TCM expert, we can only use information as a guideline. So, buy organic whenever possible, drink two-percent or whole milk at trials, where you're likely to burn off the extra calories anyway, and balance your diet to include proteins from dairy, meats and plants.

Nuts. Almost every nut has a specific benefit. Some of the best for reducing stress depleted nutrients are walnuts and Brazilian nuts. Walnuts are high in B vitamins and contain significant omega-3 fatty acids. Almonds are high in vitamin E, B1, B2, B3, B9 and are rich in minerals like manganese, magnesium, copper, phosphorus, iron, zinc and potassium. Peanuts – actually a dried legume, not a true nut – are high in vitamin B9 and B3. Pistachios are packed with nutrients, fiber and vitamins. You can also chew up cashews, macadamias (highest in fat), pecans or pine nuts.

For trial day snacking, Kathleen and I almost always mix up a bag of G.O.R.P. – Good Old-fashioned Raisins and Peanuts. With a few substitutions, like dried cherries or cranberries for raisins or cashews for peanuts, we have a fabulous, nutritious snack on hand for every trial. We also like to add dark or white chocolate chips or dark chocolate covered nuts (walnut or almonds) for variety.

Oats. Oatmeal and oat bran are significant source of dietary fiber. This fiber contains a mixture of about half soluble and half insoluble fibers. One of the soluble fiber components is beta-glucans, which has proven effective in lowering blood cholesterol. Oats also contain a variety of B vitamins and multiple amino acids, including tryptophan, arginine, glutamic acid and leucine. Melatonin is also found in oats.

Although oatmeal is not exactly a trial-friendly food, oatmeal cookies or oat bran muffins are superb travelers! Add walnuts, raisins, dried cherries, or dark chocolate chips to your recipes for more necessary nutrients on trial days.

Omega-3. Although not a "food", Omega-3 bears discussion. One of two essential fatty acids, omega-3 ingestion triggers the secretion of prostaglandin, a hormone-like substance that regulates the functioning of our immune system and fights stress. As noted previously, American diets are typically high in Omega-6 fatty acids. This has disrupted the balance between Omega-3 and Omega-6 fats. Unlike Omega-6 fats, the food sources of Omega-3 are limited. The richest source of Omega-3's are cold-water fishes, such as salmon, tuna, and mackerel. Vegetarian sources consist of green, leafy vegetables, such as spinach and broccoli. Certain vegetable oils, like flaxseed and canola oil, are also good sources.

Oranges. Nervous? Eat an orange. In one study, people who consumed a 1,000 mg of vitamin C before giving a speech had lower levels of cortisol and lower blood pressure than those who were not given the vitamin supplement. Vitamin C also has excellent antioxidant properties. Oranges, tangerines, and clementines are considered to be cooling foods in TCM. They are also extremely portable and can easily be added to smoothies and salads.

All winter while teaching lessons and at trials, I snack on clementines. Not only do I get an emotional boost and a huge dose of antioxidants, but the aroma of the orange helps everyone in class. Orange scent is an energy raiser for most people.

Sunflower seeds. Looking for a healthy snack? A handful of sunflower seeds will take care of your hunger, while enhancing your health by supplying significant amounts of vitamin E, vitamin B, magnesium and selenium. These small seeds provide lots of health benefits. The vitamin E travels throughout the body neutralizing free radicals and the magnesium is necessary for healthy bones and energy production. Sunflower seeds are also a natural source of melatonin.

Peppermint. Available in many different forms, peppermint is useful for calming your digestive tract when consumed and may relieve tension headaches when applied to the skin. TCM considers it a cooling food. Peppermint scent is also energizing for many people. So, stick a few peppermint candies in your pocket for the next time you feel your nerves reach your stomach or cause heartburn. You can also add peppermint oil as a flavor to some recipes.

Turkey. Like milk, turkey is a good source of tryptophan. Tryptophan is an essential amino acid. Although it can make you drowsy, it also aids in the production of the neurotransmitter serotonin, which calms and helps regulate feelings. Production of serotonin can elevate your mood and ward off depression. Serotonin also helps promote adequate sleep. Combining tryptophan-containing foods with complex carbohydrates, such as whole grains, increases absorption and aids in the production of serotonin. In addition to turkey, high levels of tryptophan are found in shrimp, spinach, chicken, tuna, soybeans, milk, salmon, and eggs. Vegetables like asparagus, broccoli, and cauliflower are also great tryptophan sources.

Magnesium

About two-thirds of the magnesium in the human body is found in our bones. Some helps give bones their physical structure, while the rest is found on the surface of the bone where it is stored for future use. Magnesium counterbalances calcium, which helps both nerves and muscles. In many nerve cells, magnesium blocks calcium. By blocking calcium, magnesium keeps our nerves (and the muscles they activate) relaxed. Athletes should keep an eye on their magnesium levels.

Yogurt. Have you noticed that the yogurt section of most grocery stores has practically taken over the dairy aisle? It's getting harder to find more traditional dairy foods, such as cottage cheese and sour cream, amid the sea of yogurt options. But it only makes sense that a food with as many health benefits as yogurt be given prime real estate in the supermarket. Yogurt eaters get a dose of animal protein (about 9 grams per 6-ounce serving), plus several other nutrients found in dairy foods, like calcium, vitamin B-2, B-12, potassium, and magnesium. It also contains probiotics (good bacteria that aid digestion). For trial days, freeze your yogurt the night before. It'll stay cold all morning and will be just right for a mid-morning snack. Stir in fruit, nuts, or dark chocolate chips for a great lunch.

Continuous effort – not strength or intelligence –
is the key to unlocking our potential.
~Winston Churchill

Pack Your Food

When you are on the road or at a competition for an entire day, it is important to pack your own food. Fatigue is deadly for good food choices. When you leave an event tired and end up having to grab dinner on the go, it is much harder to eat healthy. There are too many bad choices on restaurant menus and fast food is an easy choice when you are rushed, tired or disappointed. Furthermore, most trial vendors offer high-carb, low nutrient food choices because they are easy to make and profitable for the host club. Avoiding a trial diet is critical to maintaining your mental focus.

It is also important to know which direction your energy level needs to go: up or down. In the early morning hours, you may need juice or a bowl of fruit with a morning coffee to get you moving and concentrating. I am totally dysfunctional before caffeine. Later in the morning, deciding on a course strategy or working through your heeling pattern, you need nerves that are rock steady. Consuming oatmeal cookies, a turkey wrap, or a handful of homemade trail mix can provide the nutrients you need to calm your mind and focus. Selections offered at the trial or nearest convenience store are not generally the best options for maintaining an optimal energy level. Take a variety of foods so you can feed the right mood!

Taking a Bite out of Life

As I sit here, enjoying the first ice pop of the summer, I'm starting to wonder when my life stopped making sense or rather if it ever did. Okay, let's be real, it never did. It's just a bit more evident now. While I'm both baffled by my own journey – and enjoy befuddling others along the way – it seems as though a few wonderful coincidences have slowly fallen into place on the path in front of me. I'm not always sure how the cookie is going to crumble when I bite it, but I do know that I really love cookies. So, why not take a few more bites or a big one?

I'm starting to get addicted to all this adventuring. The places my little Heart Lake shelties have taken me in just the past week are incredible and that's just the icing on the cake. I know we have a ways to go and don't quite know where we are always going but I don't think we'll be turning around anytime soon!

It's funny though. Every time we hit a fork in the road, it's not a matter of which path leads to success but more about which will be more adventuresome. As I grow as a trainer and competitor, I'm learning that these adventures aren't really about success. They're about enjoying the ride, being able to take something from each experience, even when I bite off more than I can chew. Sometimes it's been best to swallow my pride, avoid talking with my mouth full, and just learn next time to take a slightly smaller bite – maybe.

Agility & Beyond Blog - Kathleen Oswald - June 28, 2013

Color

Color is a powerful psychological tool. The colors you wear and surround yourself with have a powerful effect on how you feel and on how others respond to you. Color contains a distinct message, whether you are wearing it or looking at it. Designers of clothing, houses, business spaces, and web pages know that colors influence mood. A large part of Feng Shui is to balance the colors within a room or space.

By choosing the right colors, you can directly alter your mood and energy state. While perceptions of color are somewhat subjective, there are some color effects that have universal meaning in Western cultures. For example, the red area of the color spectrum is known as warm while the opposite side of the color spectrum – blue/green - is considered cool. Regardless of society's interpretation of the color, we need to recognize that color is closely linked to emotion. Colors affect our moods and energy levels and send constant messages to those around us. What we see and what others see on us (or around us) has a subtle impact on our mental and physical state.

> *Color choice directly affects your mood and energy. What you are wearing says a lot about how you feel.*

Consider carefully what colors you wear in practice and in competition. Every color choice will invoke a response from those around you – competitors, friends and judges. This is particularly important for rally and obedience. For example, a bright red shirt worn at a major tournament is like a red-flag waved at a bull! You will invoke an extremely strong reaction from the highly competitive handlers trialing with you. On the other hand, a dark blue or green shirt will send calming messages. Which would you prefer…a calm, lazy opponent or a hyper-competitive one? Another example of color use at trials is to manipulate your energy message. If you have a methodical working dog, use warm, vibrant colors to jazz up your look. If you have a high-energy dog, use cool, calm colors to present and feel smoothness and control. You can start working on your Open score at your closet door!

Much like aromatherapy, everyone links colors with memories. If you link the bright-red of emergency vehicles to a traumatic experience, your response to red will be significantly different than the individual who links that color to a special Valentine's Day gift. Surround yourself with colors that please you and invoke a strong positive emotion. Furthermore, color choices are not limited to clothing. The color of your dog's collar and leash, your chair, soft-crate, umbrella, car interior, and hotel room can all impact your mood.

> Knowledge has to be improved, challenged, and increased constantly, or it disappears.
> ~ Peter Drucker

Color Combinations

How you combine colors is also important. There are three color schemes:

Monochromatic. This uses a single color in varying shades. It presents a clean, interesting picture that is soothing and pleasing to the eye. Combine the different shades with enough variation so you avoid being boring or plain. For example, when using black, mix with charcoal and silver. If you are using brown, add accents with gold or tan. If you like purple, add a touch of pink or combine with a soft blue.

Complimentary. Select colors directly opposite from one another on the color wheel. For example, use red and green or blue and yellow. This automatically puts a cool color (green-blue-purple) with a warm color (yellow-orange-red-pink). This is a popular color scheme with sports teams. It suggests both aggression/strength and cool, calm, and collected!

Triple colors, Select three colors equally spaced around the color wheel. For example, use red, blue and yellow or pink, turquoise and gold. Triple color schemes are popular with advertisers and fashion designers to get a significant pop of color. The color pop demands a response from its audience. You will definitely be memorable.

Color Selection

Since colors are individual choices, there are no right-or-wrong choices for what you wear or what colors you surround yourself with. It all comes down to awareness. Take time to appreciate the color's impact on your emotions when you are shopping for trial gear and clothing. It is also a good idea to have a variety of color choices. All purple is a great personal theme but purple might not always match the attitude you need to adopt or the message you want to send to a judge or other competitors!

Your color choices and some messages to keep in mind.....

Purple. Purple is associated with wealth, prosperity, royalty and rich sophistication. This color stimulates the brain activity used in problem solving. Touches of purple lend an air of mystery, wisdom, and respect. It is also feminine and romantic. It is a complex color invoking thoughts of abundance (plums and grapes), spirituality, nobility (royal purple velvet), ceremony, mystery (wizard capes), transformation, wisdom, enlightenment, cruelty, arrogance, and mourning. Purple is considered an exotic color that is a favorite of highly creative people. I frequently select a purple shirt when teaching agility seminars.

Lavender. Light purple or Lavender is associated with healing, calming and renewal. It is a softer choice than deep purple. It also mixes well with other colors.

Blue. Ask people their favorite color and a clear majority will say blue. The natural world, from sky to ocean, surrounds us in blue. Over time, blue has become associated with reliability (e.g., blue business suit), stability, intelligence, and loyalty. Many uniforms – policemen, Marines, postal service - are dark blue. Seeing the color blue actually causes your body to produce chemicals that are calming. It can slow the pulse rate, lower body temperature, and reduce appetite. People tend to be more productive in a blue room because they are calm and focused on the task at hand. Guess what color my office is painted! Kathleen frequently selects dark blue to wear at major tournaments.

Blue can be strong and steadfast or light and friendly, depending on the hue. Fashion consultants recommend wearing blue to job interviews. You appear warm, down to earth, and dependable. The impact of blue extends also to turquoise, teal, aqua and aquamarine. At large national events, I select blue for the first trial day. We always reconnect with our agility friends and competitors from around the country and I want to appear approachable and calm. A cool color choice sets a friendly tone. The time to appear aggressive and strong is on the last day in the Finals!

Green. Green is life. Abundant in nature, green signifies growth, renewal, health, and environment. It is a calming color that's very pleasing to the senses and yet energizing. Dark forest green is associated with terms like conservative, masculine, and wealth. It is also the color associated with money, good luck (shamrocks), generosity and fertility. Green invokes thoughts of Irish meadows, grass, spring, sage, pine, and vegetables from celery to lettuce to cucumbers to broccoli. On the flip side, green is jealousy or envy (green-eyed monster) and inexperience.

Green is a restful color with the same calming attributes of blue. Green calms nerves and balances the whole body particularly when used in several different shades. People waiting to appear on TV sit in "green rooms" to relax them. Surgeons and hospitals often use green because it relaxes patients. Brides in the Middle Ages wore green to symbolize fertility.

Mix green with black to send a message of calm and power or mix dark green with gold to win with calm assurance.

Brown. This is the color of the earth itself and what could represent stability better. It is associated with things being natural and solid. Light brown implies genuineness while dark brown represent strength and stability (think wood and/or leather). Brown is no longer just for men. It's a new favorite for women. Beige, tan and camel are also associated with stability.

Clothing for obedience trials tends to be brown or black. Remember though that brown projects stability not winner! If tan or light brown is your choice for pants or shirt, add touches of orange for energy or gold to project being "number one."

Yellow. Cheerful yellow is the color of the sun and is strongly associated with laughter, happiness (think Smiley face) and good times. A person surrounded by yellow feels optimistic because the brain actually releases more serotonin when around this color. It is the color associated with optimism. Bright, sunny yellow is an attention getter. It has the power to speed up our metabolism and bring out some creative thoughts (legal tablets are yellow for good reason) though some shades of yellow are associated with cowardice. Yellow is seldom – if ever – used by professional sports teams unless it is paired with lots of menacing black!

The colors you wear and surround yourself with have a powerful effect on how you feel and on how others respond to you.

Deep yellow or gold is definitely a good shade to use in competitions that are judged. Gold is linked to celebration (holidays, champagne), winning and wealth. Why not wear the gold-medal color into the ring? Dark yellows appear positive and friendly while pastel hues are calm, gentle, and non-threatening.

This is another color that I select when doing seminars, particularly when I do not know the students attending. A pale yellow sweatshirt or shirt projects a friendly energy which helps the students engage with me and my lesson. Bright yellow is a common team shirt at agility competitions. Particularly when used with blue and green text and images, it sends the message, "Pay attention to us we're good but we're friendly too!"

Orange. The most flamboyant color on the planet! It's the color most associated with fun times, happy and energetic days. It is a warm color often linked to the abundance of fall (pumpkins, squash, carrots). It is also associated with ambition. There is nothing remotely calm about this color. Orange is used for attention-getting purposes, such as on caution signs. It symbolizes warmth (fires glow orange), enthusiasm, flamboyancy, and demands attention. Used in small touches, it can jazz up any of the calming colors like dark blue, green or brown. It is a common choice for athletic team uniforms as an accent color or full-blown color scheme. It is very popular in the NFL.

The soul becomes dyed with
the color of its thoughts.
~Marcus Aurelius

Pink. Pink is another calming color. Sports teams sometimes paint the opposing team's locker room pale pink to keep the players passive and less energetic. It is a feminine color and is has powerful associations in some shades. It is the color for infant girls and breast cancer. Think of pink as the color of romance, love and gentle feelings. Pink hues range from soothing to mildly energizing. In the professional sports world, pink seems to appear more often in individual sports, like tennis and golf, than in team sports.

Red. Red is the color of energy. It's associated with movement and excitement and draws the eye immediately. Wearing red clothes will make you noticeable. Red is the symbol of life (blood is red) and is used at holidays (Christmas, Valentine's Day) that are about love and giving. The most emotionally intense color, red stimulates a faster heartbeat and breathing. Since it is an extreme color, red is also the color of aggression and danger. It is extremely popular with all the American sports leagues from the NFL to NBA to NHL! It is the warmest and most energetic color in the spectrum. It should also be used carefully in a competitive environment that is judged. You are projecting aggression with a red shirt or jacket. Be sure that you wish to be marked as "the one to beat" when you wear it! Tiger Woods always wears red and black on the final day of a golf tournament.

White. For most of the world, this is the color associated with purity (wedding dresses) and cleanliness (doctors in white coats). It is neutral and yet invokes creativity (white boards, blank slates). It is a compression of all the colors in the color spectrum and is in perfect balance. It represents reverence, purity, simplicity, cleanliness, peace, humility, precision, innocence, youth, birth, cold (winter snow and ice), good, sterility, and marriage. We associate white with the good guy.

It can also be hard to wear around our four-pawed pals or at outdoor events! If you want to wear white, try using it as an accent or image/text color.

Black. Black is the absence of light and, thus, color. It represents both power/strength and evil. In folklore, villains and witches are frequently depicted wearing black. It is also the color of authority and intelligence (e.g., higher-education graduation robes are black; black box analysis; and black tuxedos or suits). Black also implies sadness, remorse, mourning and death, particularly in the Western hemisphere.

It is a serious color that evokes strong emotions and sets or sends vastly different messages depending on the color mix. Wearing black creates the image of being in control or on a mission. This impression extends to charcoal, medium and dark gray. It is popular in fashion because it makes people appear leaner and in sportswear, it gives the appearance of strength. Hence, the overuse of black by professional and collegiate athletic teams trying to intimidate their opponents. Black can also be teamed with a cool color to send a mixed message. Black blended with dark green or blue projects strength and calmness. Black with red projects both strength and aggression. Black with yellow sends the very mixed message of strength and friendliness.

Gray. Gray is a neutral, balanced color. It is a cool, conservative color that seldom evokes strong emotion although it can be seen as a cloudy or moody if overused. Gray suits are part of the uniform of the corporate world. Some shades of gray are associated with old age, death, or a sense of loss. Dark, charcoal gray carries with it some of the strength of black. It is a sophisticated color and can be paired with many colors. Silver is often associated with strong character (sterling in-fact), a celebration, or money (coins).

Accessories

It is not just your shirt, jacket or pants that can be considered for color. Think about using bracelets, gloves, scarves, buttons, belts, shoes and shoelaces. It is important to look down or in the mirror and see colors that inspire you. I frequently use a watch and bracelets. Kathleen likes shoes and shoelaces to enhance her attitude and focus. In recent years, athletic shoe lines make for great fun with all their unique and highly decorative color mixes.

Touch

Much like breathing, touch is an extremely strong tool for altering your energy level and gaining control over your conscious mind. Smell and sight have a subtle effect. Sound has a direct impact, as does nutrition. In stressful situations, however, the two strongest and quickest tools for calming your mind are breath control and touch or stretching. Although discussed last, it is important to remember how powerful touch and stretching are.

Both touching drills and the stretching exercises engage your muscles and the motion engages your mind. The body-mind link produces immediate calm and allows the mind to focus.

Touch Exercises

Any rhythmic touch can relax your mind. As a child, we were taught to stay quiet in class or church by rolling your thumbs. It's a good finger exercise but hard to do while holding a leash! Yoga practitioners use finger push-ups for calm. The five-finger Qigong exercise, which combines both touch and breathing, is extremely useful for relaxing and calming the mind.

You can also use worry beads or Baoding balls for stress relief. Worry beads are a simple fix for nervous energy and jittery thoughts. Many cultures have some form of worry beads, which are non-religious. A worry bead string consists of a loose loop of beads that are handled in several ways. The beads are rhythmically counted, clicked gently onto the shield bead, or swung thru loops. Beads are often made of natural minerals or metal to improve the tactile sensation. Baoding balls, otherwise known as Chinese exercise balls, consist of a two metal, hollow spheres one inside the other with a chime in between. Rolling or rotating two of the Baoding balls in the palm of your  hand without the balls touching takes practice. However, once mastered it keeps the mind occupied with a steady, rhythmic motion, which is very meditative.

Although useful stress reducers, worry beads and Baoding balls are not the best choice while you are waiting with your dog outside the ring or field. The following two exercises can be done anywhere and are simple enough to do while you are waiting with your dog.

- Touch counting

- Tongue press

- Jaw stretch

Much like thumb rolling, worry bead clicking, or yoga finger push-ups, these simple exercises work by focusing your mind on a specific task. The repetitive nature of the task releases tension and naturally settles your breathing. Similar to the breath counting exercise, touch activities require concentration to maintain the counts. This keeps your conscious mind occupied and it cannot stay anxious and worried.

Furthermore, small motor exercises work well at trials where you frequently have no space and are in a rush. Maintaining mental control in the two minutes before you enter the ring or test area is absolutely critical! Touch exercises give you control in those last critical moments. You can do any of these exercises while waiting with your dog and no one will even notice.

Trust yourself, you know more than you think you do.
~Benjamin Spock

Touch Counting.

There are many small touch exercises and you can easily create your own. One of my favorites is touch counting. I work this exercise while waiting for my turn in the ring and also when stuck in annoying airport lines.

For the first few times through this exercise, hold your right hand palm up with your fingers gently curled. We use the right hand to help control and fully occupy the left-brain. Once you are proficient, you can do with your hand at your side. During the learning phase, do at least twice a day for several cycles. With repetition, you can extend to as many cycles as necessary to calm your mind.

Exercise Steps

1 - Hold your right hand with your palm facing you and gently touch each finger to the thumb pad. Start with your index finger and end with your pinkie for four touches. Repeat the four touches backward, start with pinkie and end with index finger. Make each touch distinct. Press gently and methodically for all eight touches total in the first cycle.

2 - Repeat the touch pattern (index to pinkie and pinkie to index) but do two touches per finger on your thumb pad.

3 - Repeat the touch pattern with three touches per finger on thumb pad.

4 - Repeat the touch pattern with four touches per finger on thumb pad.

As you work the touch pattern, be aware of a long, deep breath. You may feel your shoulders relax as your mind calms and your body releases tension in the neck and back.

Without knowledge action is useless and knowledge without action is futile.
~Abu Bakr

Tongue Press

This is the easiest of all the *muscles-over-mind* exercises and you can do it anywhere. Simply open your jaw slightly, enough to unalign your front teeth. Gently press your tongue to the back of the top teeth. This very natural position and it is instantly calming as it releases tension from the mouth and jaw. You may immediately feel yourself sinking into a long, deep breath.

In a stressful situation, use the tongue press to release tension and trigger deeper breathing. Even without inducing deeper breathing, you will benefit from unclenching your jaws!

Jaw Stretch

Relaxing your jaw is beneficial in many situations. It is an easy exercise to relax and stretch the jaw muscles.

Exercise Steps

1 - Place finger tips gently on the jaw joint. Press gently, but firmly to loosen the joint. A few simple circles should begin to relax the muscles.

2 - Open your jaw as far as possible without causing discomfort or pain. Hold for a five seconds.

3 - Close your jaw and clench for three seconds

4 - Repeat the open for five seconds, close for three seconds Do two to ten rotations. If you feel the need to take a deep breath during or between sets, relax and let yourself enjoy a deep, tension-reducing breath.

5 - Finish with another brief finger tip massage of the jaw joint. Press gently, but firmly to loosen the muscles. Use a small circular motion.

As you work to loosen the jaw muscles, you may also release enough tension to induce a jaw stretch. If this happens, let the stretch finish. A natural stretch is an excellent indication of stress-reduction!

Stretching

Stretching is your body's way of releasing stress. Tight muscles naturally want to stretch and relax. By consciously releasing this tension, you can alter your physical state. It is also equally energizing.

A full body stretch can be a major stress reducer. You are directly linking your mind to your body. The focus on the body and specific muscles will force your mind into a calmer state. Often we hold tension in our muscles without even being aware of the tension build-up. Stretching is a great addition to your competition routine. It can also ease your transition from work mode to dog training mode. Dragging work, school, or family stress into your training sessions is counterproductive. Five minutes of stretching can eliminate this problem.

Use this routine before practice sessions or even as a stress-reducer before you go to bed. It will make you comfortable with the stretch sequences and positions and then the routine will be familiar and easy to use at trials and tournaments. My trial routine incorporates several minutes of serious stretching right after I put on my agility shoes and before I get the video camera, treats, and the dog. This lets me focus on the motions and remove any lingering tension before I connect with my canine partner.

For a full body stretch, start at the top (head) and move steadily down (feet).

Shoulders. Release shoulder tension with shoulder rolls. Roll shoulders forward three times and then roll three times backward. Make the motion a big circle. Think about drawing your shoulders up toward ears and then forward or back.

Neck. With relaxed shoulders, you can move onto the neck. Drop your head gently forward – chin to chest. Circle head clockwise to the right, then back, then left and end with chin down. Repeat two more times for a full three circles. Repeat circles counterclockwise. Do three.

Upper Back. Place left arm across the front of your body at chest height. Place your right forearm on the outside of your left arm, just above the elbow and pull into your body. This is like hugging your left arm to your upper chest. As you pull in, you should feel muscles in shoulder and back stretch. Repeat on the right arm.

Arms. For the arm, stretch your left arm out straight with wrist up, palm out and fingers down. With your right hand, gently pull hand back toward your body. You should feel the stretch in your left forearm. Repeat stretch on the right arm.

Lower Back. For a full back stretch, stand with your feet at shoulder width or slightly wider. Place your hands, palm down on your thighs. Slowly slide your hands down your legs from thigh to knee to shin to ankles to tops of feet and then to floor. Stop when your back is stretching. Hold for 25 seconds. Stand up slowly and then repeat. This position should also stretch your hamstrings (back of thighs).

Hips. You can loosen your knees and hips with gentle circles. For hip circles, stand with your feet at shoulder width and place your hands on your hips. Roll your hips in a circle. Do three circles clockwise and three counter-clockwise. For knee circles, stand with your feet about six-inches apart and put your hands on your knees. Circle knees three times clockwise and three times counter-clockwise.

Thighs. In order to stretch your quads (front of thighs), hold onto the back of a chair or some solid object with your left hand. Lift your right foot toward your rear-end. As your foot comes up, gently grab the top of the foot and pull your heel into your rear-end. Hold for 20 seconds. Continue holding in that position and arch your back slightly. This will engage your hip flexors in a gentle stretch. Hold for 20 seconds. Repeat on the left side.

Calves. For a calf stretch, hold the back of a chair or lean into a solid object. Place your left foot slightly forward and keep your left knee bent. Place your right foot at shoulder width about two feet behind you. There are two calf stretches. For the first one, stretch your right heel toward the ground. You should feel your calf stretch. To deepen the stretch, keep your hands on the back of the chair while you lift your shoulders. This should put a slight arch in your back which aids the calf stretch. For the second stretch, maintain the same position but this time bend the right knee slightly. Keep your heel on the floor and sink your weight onto the bent knee.

A few quick notes about stretching exercises…
- never bounce, just stretch
- stretch your muscles gently, don't push to the point of pain
- frequent stretch is better than one long, painful session
- get help from a physical therapist or trainer if you have no range of motion or an injury

Conclusion

You now have six distinct methods to move your conscious mind from anxious or worried to calm. Remember you cannot *think* yourself calm. Each of the six body-mind links...

- breathing
- aromatherapy
- music
- nutrition
- color
- touch and stretch

interact and create an environment that lets your body influence your mind's state. Within each method, there are multiple skills that must be developed and explored before you need them in competition. Some will be easy to learn and adopt. Others require some practice.

As you begin to use the *muscles-over-mind* program, your awareness of your energy state will improve. Once this happens you can truly explore the different tools and figure out what works best for you and – equally important – when to use them. It is also critical to remember that each method can be used to either calm or energize the conscious mind.

And, the best of it....when you have control you can go anywhere!

MACH6 Demon & MACH3 Jenna in September 2012

We: A Journey I Didn't Plan

I am two years down a road I never thought I would travel. And yet, looking back, it was one of the best decisions I've ever made. Two years ago, I started working with a special dog, a Doberman called Nikki. At first, we had trouble staying in sync. We had trouble trying to make time. We had trouble trying to stay focused. We were scared of the judge and the ring crew. We couldn't find the weave entry. We didn't always like to take the jumps.

Now I say "we" because Nikki and I are a team. All of our successes, all of our failures, we share. All of the issues we've overcome are a combined effort; this is a journey we are taking together. I've come to find many people in this sport, to whom the dog is not an equal. When something goes wrong, it's the dog's fault. When something goes right, it's the handler/trainer's success alone. I'm so proud to say that on our journey together Nikki and I really have become a team. If nothing else comes from our time together, our bond will be something I will always cherish. All the lessons we've learned, and with so many ups and downs along the way, every moment has been truly worth it. There was once a time when Nikki didn't enjoy the game. I'm so very happy to say that now I can see her having as much fun as I am. Her eyes light up when we run and she is excited to go in the ring with me. We are now half way to a PACH. We are *almost* qualified for AKC 2014 Nationals. We have perfect weekends. We stay focused on course. We take all the jumps, sometimes extra for fun. We love the game.

Thank you so much Nikki, for letting me be part of this team, it has challenged me in so many ways, and you have made me a better person.

Agility & Beyond Blog - Kathleen Oswald - October 10, 2013

Post Script - March 2014
Not only did we qualify for the AKC Agility Nationals, we finished 2nd in the 20"
Preferred Class. And, exactly seven days later, we completed our seventh
consecutive double Q to complete our PACH and PAX. God bless you Nikki – and
your owner Elaine – for letting me share this adventure with you.

Jenna – Overseeing lessons in the yard

#2
Centered
Mind

The second "C" of success is a centered mind. Once your mind is calm, you have an opportunity to live moment-to-moment or centered on yourself. Without a past or a future, your mind cannot judge or compare or analyze. There is only now. A quiet mind just exists. It is aware but does not judge. In the present moment, there is no right or wrong. Life just is. A calm conscious mind can remain in the present moment, which allows it to remain focused and quiet.

All of this sounds very zen but a centered conscious mind is not just for yoga, meditation or new age groupies. Achieving extraordinary athletic performances on command requires that your mind be locked in the present.

A few key points about being centered in the present moment….

The Zone. Today, we have a term for living in the present moment. It is *The Zone*. Athletes who can move into the present moment and remain there throughout a competitive event have a tremendous advantage. The Zone is just the present. It is not some extreme state of mind accessed only by shamans, meditation gurus or professional athletes with million dollar contracts. Existing in the present moment – in the zone – is possible for anyone and it is possible to achieve when you want. It is does require some training, or for most adults, some retraining.

Present moment existence. You have had plenty of practice living in the present moment. As a young child, you lived there pretty much all the time. Young children can't tell time so they have no schedules. They don't count very high so ten minutes is forever; plenty of time to take out another set of toys and start a whole new game. Young children want everything in the present timeframe. They don't want a cookie after their nap. They want it now!

The good news is that you can turn back the clock. You can learn to live – for short periods – in the *now* moment. As adults with responsibilities and schedules obviously you cannot stay there all day. However, with practice you can train your mind to stay in the present for the duration of your Utility test, hunt test or a masters agility course.

Rejoice in the things that are present,
all else is beyond thee.
~ Montaigne

Conscious mind resistance. Your conscious mind, of course, wants to be anywhere but in the present moment. It is BORING for your conscious mind. There is nothing for it to do! Your conscious mind's power is in judging, comparing, analyzing and predicting. It is a power that wants to be utilized. Your conscious mind desperately needs to analyze the past and dream about the future. The centered existence of a present-focused mind requires nothing from the conscious mind so it is constantly looking to escape.

Body and subconscious mind. While your conscious mind thrives on moving effortlessly from past-to-present-to-future, your body and your subconscious mind can only exist in the present. They are fully grounded in this moment. Think about it, your heartbeat cannot be in the past. Your subconscious mind cannot monitor your digestive system in the future. Thus, every time your thoughts shift from the present, you lose the connections to your body and subconscious mind. Obviously, this is not a problem day-to-day. In fact, the sub-second, circular thought shifts of your mind from present-to-future-to-past-to-present are a powerful tool that cannot be matched even by today's mega supercomputers. It is, however, a handicap when you are heeling thru an off-leash figure-8 and your feet are no longer linked to your conscious mind!

Thought jumps. Every time your conscious mind regains control and yanks you out of the present moment there are two directions your mind can go: backward into the past or forward into the future. Without control, either of these jumps can be extremely counterproductive. With every thought jump, fear and doubt are given an opportunity to swamp your mind and to hijack your thoughts.

The Past. Unfortunately, many forays into the past are devastating to the success of the current moment. Mental time travel into the past frequently involves revisiting mistakes and failures, which deposit doubt and fear right into the present moment. Walking around a trial, early in the morning I hear comments from fellow competitors and students that scream of fear, doubt and negativity.

> *At a competition, you must be extremely vigilant over your thoughts. Negative thoughts and daydreams at an event are particularly destructive.*

I should have stayed in bed. My dog never finds the go-out in this building.

No parking. No crate space. No food vendor. Why am I here?

My dog is definitely gonna blow that tunnel/dog walk discrimination.

Well today is a wash. I've never qualified under this judge.

Really! At seven thirty in the morning, I hear this and usually have to resist escorting these people back to their cars for an express trip back home or ship them off to the mall or anywhere other than a dog trial! Before the day has even begun, before they've leashed their dog or put on their competition shoes, they've allowed fear and doubt to sabotage the potential for success and enjoyment. Their past has already determined their future! These competitors need to regain mental control before their uncontrolled dip into past problems or mistakes ruins the day.

On the other hand, a controlled trip into the past can be a major mental boost. Redirecting a negative thought stream to remind themselves of past triumphs over adversity can be very productive. Spending a few moments reliving recent successes or selecting an aspect of the day to enjoy can raise confidence

The Future. The same control is also required when dealing with the future. Taking a plunge into the "What If" world of the future can be productive – creating confidence and expanding your comfort zone with dreams of future success. However, the "What If" world can also deteriorate into gloom and doom scenarios that feature catastrophic failure, embarrassment and humiliation. Playing in the future requires serious thought control. Dreams of glory are fantastic mental preps. Daydreaming about failure is destructive and unproductive. You must be particularly aware of traveling into the future – savoring a victory – during an event. It is a surefire way to blow a successful performance. Your mind may be thinking "We just won!" but your feet, hands and canine partner are in the present with work still to do.

Uncontrolled thought jumps into the past or future inhibit top-dog performances. Learning to manage these shifts from present-to-future or-past is a critical skill. With the focus tools in this section, you can learn to gently guide your mind back into the present and let negative emotions vaporize.

Your dog's mind. Our dogs live their entire lives in the present moment. We firmly believe this is a huge part of their appeal to us. When we interact with our dogs, we live in the present moment with them. Think about how time flies when you are training, playing or walking with your dog. As dog trainers and competitors, our best training sessions and trial days occur when we move into our dog's frame of existence. They cannot move into the future with you nor can they go backward into the past. Living with them in the present is healthy – both mentally and physically!

The most effective way to do it, is to do it.
~Amelia Earhart

Now that we've indentified the advantages of living with a centered, calm mind, it is time to examine how to maintain a present-focused mind. The following section describe the tools you need to relearn the skill of moment-to-moment living. We then examine how to get into and stay in the present moment, even during the stress and tension of a trial or competitive training session, using triggers and key phrases.

- Present Moment Living

- Create a Centering Trigger

- Create a Key Phrase

> Ninety percent of my game is mental.
> It's my concentration that has gotten me this far.
> ~ Chris Evert

Present Moment Living

Most adults do not spend much time in the present moment. In the modern world, it is something of a luxury. We are all encouraged – frequently rewarded – for Type A personality behaviors. Doing two, three or even four things at once is normal. In reality, today's expectations for multi-tasking are a bit outrageous. We are supposed to learn a new language while driving to work. While watching TV, you should be posting on Facebook or Tweeting about the show. During commercials, you should be able to pay all your bills on-line while the popcorn is in the microwave. Jogging or hiking? Shouldn't you be listening to all the classics that you avoided in high school? Stopped for your morning coffee? With free WiFi access, surely you can get ahead of the day's work by answering half dozen emails while waiting in line for your latte. And so the day goes on. If you can do one thing, then you can do two or three.

Quiet time is a foreign concept in our I-pod-driven, internet-access-everywhere life styles. Single-task focus is mostly extinct in Western society. Access to the mental power of single-task focus is now reserved for trying to fall asleep. Yes indeed. Our conscious minds are so frenetic, we now have to focus on actively shutting down our thoughts enough to fall asleep. Yikes!

So, for many adults, the first task is actually to get their wired-up brain to acknowledge that the present is an actual state of mind. The second task is to practice staying in that present moment for more than an instant. And, finally as a competitive athlete, you need to maintain your present-state focus surrounded by all the distractions of a competitive environment.

As adults, we need to relearn the skill of present-moment living. We must go back and relearn the joy of focusing on one task or one thought for as long as we like or for the duration of an activity.

You cannot just say "mind focus on this." Even saying "Focus!" with authority does not mean that your mind can or will comply. Like any other skill – from course analysis to heeling to disc tossing – you must practice. The following exercises work on getting your mind into the present. They start simple and become more advanced as you gain proficiency. With a few minutes each day, you can quickly retrain your mind to remain in the present for several minutes. An excellent goal is to move toward five or ten minutes.

As you gain success at present-moment living, you then need to change the level of distractions. There is a huge difference between running a focus drill sitting in a comfy soft chair in your family room versus entering the ring at the National Championships! With our students, we tackle the process using three distinct levels.

Level 1 - Mild. When you begin working your present-moment exercises, start with low level or mild distractions. Do the simple exercises (word counting, number sequencing, and an object focus) in a relatively quiet location without motion or sound distractions. Sit on a park bench or picnic table. Setup a comfortable chair in a silent room or with a soft background music (beach waves, bird songs, etc) playing or use a quiet spot in a park or your yard.

Level 2 - Moderate. As you learn to hold your mind in the present moment for a minute or so, you can increase your mind's controllability by using mild or moderate distractions in the environment. For example, do the object focus exercise while stuck in traffic or with the TV on a low volume. Can you block out the sound of the TV show? How about during a commercial? Commercials are deliberately aimed at getting your attention so they make excellent proving grounds for mental focus. To increase the difficulty of the quiet meditation, add both noise and motion. Sit in the food court at the mall or do while waiting for your gas tank to be filled.

Level 3 - High. The final step is to do your exercises with major distractions. Sit ringside during the Steeplechase final at an agility trial with your eyes closed. Can you maintain a calm, quiet mind? How about at the vet's office with your stressed out dog whining and squirming? This is closer to the level of present moment focus you'll need at the gate at the trial or test. You need to be calm but your dog isn't always going to be cooperative. Maintaining your present moment focus with a wired-up, excited dog is definitely a learned skill.

Focus on the journey, not the destination.
Joy is found not in finishing an activity but in doing it.
~ Greg Anderson

The following eight exercises are just to get you started. There are lots of ways and methods to keep your mind focused. As your mind learns to maintain a present-moment existence with these exercises, be gently aware of your breathing and muscle tension. Notice the release of tension and your natural, deeper breathing. You may find yourself yawning or even stretching. All of these are signals that your mind and body are synchronizing.

Word counting. This is an easy exercise that focuses the mind by forcing it to count rather than read the words in a phrase, paragraph or page of text. If your mind insists on reading, then count the words backward a few times or deliberately speed up your counting. When doing this exercise, count the words with your eyes and mind. Do not use a finger or pen tip.

Start with a short quote like the following by Robert Louis Stevenson,

> *"Don't judge each day by the harvest you reap but by the seeds that you plant."*

or a short phrase like the following from Frank Outlaw,

> *"Watch your thoughts; they become words. Watch your words; they become actions. Watch your actions; they become habits. Watch your habits; they become character. Watch your character; it becomes your destiny."*

Stuck in traffic? Count the words on a billboard advertisement. Waiting in line at a store? Count the words on the cover of a magazine. With a bit of practice, you can count words easily in a long paragraph or on a full page.

These exercises are not a word counting test. Notice that there's no answer key! They are focus practice for your conscious mind. It doesn't matter if you get an exact count. What matters is that you are able to keep your mind focused completely on counting words – don't read the words or think about the stories inside the magazine or let your mind wander off to rehash some nagging problem at work. Let your mind do one thing – count words. If it wanders, gently refocus.

Number sequencing. There are many variations of this exercise. One of the simplest is to count backward from 100 to 1. Another is to count from 1 to 100 by three's. For a sequencing exercise, you can use any multiplier (e.g., two's, three's, five's, ten's) that keeps your mind focused. Many people find that counting by two is too simple and their mind can actually wander even while counting. Counting by three's requires more mental focus for most people. However, with practice even counting by three's may become too easy. When this happens, switch to another multiplier. Try four's or seven's.

This is not a math test. If you get frustrated or lost in the counting sequence, simply start over. Remember there is no right or wrong in the present moment. Being aware that you are no longer counting successfully by three's is fine. Telling yourself that you are an idiot is a judgment and means you've shifted out of the present!

Number counting is an excellent focus drill to do while driving, waiting in line, or trying to relax enough to fall asleep. It is a useful variation on counting sheep. Of course, if it works well enough to shift you into sleep mode, do not do it while driving!

Mantras. At its simplest, a mantra or mantram is a word or phrase that is repeated over and over to clear the mind. Mantras have been used for thousands of years by many different cultures and religions for calm and/or spiritual enlightenment. Repeating a phrase has a unique effect on the human brain. The intense focus required forces your mind to let go of troubling thoughts and destructive emotions, like anger, fear and anxiety. Repetition of a mantra can actually feel like a vacation for an overworked, stressed out mind.

> **Mantras & Worry Beads**
>
> Worry beads and mantras go hand-in-hand. Click through a worry bead string or loop each time you repeat your mantra. The steady sound and motion of a bead click blends nicely with the repetition of a mantra.

The mantra can be a simple word, like Patience, Kindness, or Focus, or you can use a phrase. It can also be a multi-syllable sound such as the Hindu OM sound. Some people like to use a short affirmation as their mantra. Try one of these:

* I am present.
* I love myself.
* I am patient.

Whatever you choose, it should be short and easy to remember. Your mantra should also be positive and have meaning for you. It must be believable to you to have power. Mantras must also be repeated hundreds or thousands of times not twenty or thirty. Of course, you do not need to repeat a thousand times in a sitting!

Peak performance is meditation in motion.
~ Greg Louganis

Mental games. Simple word or math games are another easy way to move your mind into the present moment. Any game that requires mental effort forces you to concentrate, which keeps your conscious mind in the now. One of the best and most popular is Sudoku. There are also lots of traditional word games, like crosswords, scrambles, jumbles or word sleuth, available in the daily paper and many more online at sites like Facebook, Pogo™ or BigFishGames. An easy mental game for almost anywhere is to play with anagrams. Simply select a word or short phrase, and list all the possible words from those letters. Anagram play lets you be creative and focused without the pressure to be correct and solve the puzzle. Just do your best – the goal is to practice focusing not unlock the next level or beat the clock. When you are playing the game of your choice, set aside time to play and truly focus on the game. Let unrelated thoughts and pressures go by.

Task focus. Select a short, simple task such as emptying the dishwasher, throwing a ball for your dog to retrieve, brushing your teeth, cleaning a window, filling dog food bowls, setting up a dog crate, or brewing a pot of coffee. The task should be one you can repeat effortlessly without a lot of conscious thought.

Begin the exercise by taking a deep breath and standing still for a brief moment. This creates a definite beginning to the exercise. As you begin the task, focus on the job. Be aware of how you are moving and what you are doing with your hands, arms, body, feet, etc but let your mind be quiet. Do not create a task list or try to go faster or slower. Stay in the present moment. Your existence should be now. Be aware of your breathing. It should be slow and steady. If you find yourself holding your breath or breathing shallow, just take a deep breath.

As always, ignore non-task thoughts. Just let them fade from existence as you refocus on the present and notice your motions as you complete the task. End with another deep breath and a brief moment of stillness.

By focusing on the simple task, you are giving your conscious mind practice at being quiet even while actively completing a task. Remember, your conscious mind likes to multi-task. If your body can do work without interference or direction, your conscious mind firmly believes it should be thinking about something else - Facebook updates, the shopping list, why your dog chases butterflies, why there are butterflies – anything! Maintaining focus through habitual activities is a critical skill for competitive athletes. Your best performances will come when you are letting your muscles work without conscious interference but you are still focused!

Object focus. Select a small neutral object – paper clip, marble, pen cap, pine cone, leaf, quarter, flower, key, golf ball, colorful rock, safety pin, etc. Place the object in the palm of your hand. Set a timer for two minutes. Remain focused on the object for the full two minutes. Examine its shape, smell, size, edges and texture. Notice how it moves if you shift it in your palm or how it feels if you close your hand around it. Do not play with it and do not watch the time.

Ignore any non-object thoughts. Notice them and then let them float away like leaves fallen into a stream. Refocus on your object. Your conscious mind may resist this exercise. It will get bored studying a simple object for multiple minutes. When your mind wanders away from the object, gently guide it back. As your ability to focus improves, your non-object thoughts will be fewer and your refocus ability will be quicker.

Use a different object for each session. With practice, you will discover it easy to focus for two, three or more minutes. This exercise is excellent practice for your conscious mind to rediscover how to remain in the present moment.

Concentration is the secret of strength.
~ Ralph Waldo Emerson

Object visualization. Using the same object, close your eyes and visualize the small object sitting on your palm. Set a timer for one minute and concentrate on creating a sharp visual image in your mind.

Picture the object's shape, size, edges, temperature and textures. Using an unusual object – marble, small rock, leaf, plastic toy, hair clip – with lots of color and textures or an object with lots of print and different sides – AAA battery, stick of gum, key ring - will make focusing easier. Common objects – paper clips, penny, pen caps – make the exercise harder since your mind has an image and may tend to wander more. Hold your focus on *your* object versus your mind's image. This is an excellent advanced focus drill due to its increased degree of difficulty.

Keep the object in your palm and check your mental image to the real one at the end of a minute. This portion of the exercise also works your visualization skill. As always, ignore non-object thoughts. Notice them and then let them go as you refocus on the object. With practice, expand this focus exercise to two or three minutes.

Quiet awareness. Your final exercise is a short five-minute meditation. Your goal is not cosmic enlightenment. It is to achieve a state of mindfulness – awareness without thought. Even simple, short meditation sessions are exercise for your mind. It is not an escape from reality; it is an escape into reality.

Sit in a quiet room in a comfortable chair or position. You can lie down but it is easier to focus while sitting up. Set a timer for five minutes. Keep your mind free of thoughts by focusing on your breathing. It should be slow and steady. If you find yourself holding your breath or breathing shallow, just take a deep breath. Your mind cannot be blank unless you are unconscious or dead, so do not try to empty your mind. Just be aware of your surroundings. Listen to the sound of the room, house or building. Let thoughts pass through your mind without judging or analyzing them. Should your conscious mind bump you out of the present moment, simply refocus on your breathing (try not to alter it though), the soft sounds around you, or the sensations of sitting.

As always, an excellent way to stay grounded in the present is to connect your mind and body. During the five minutes, start with your toes and work to the top of your head. Notice all the physical sensations of sitting without actually moving. Are your feet warm, cold, tired, or sore? How does the chair seat feel against your legs? What does the surface of the chair feel like? Is it hard, soft, scratchy, cold? Where does it touch your body? Let your connection move up your back, shoulders, neck and head. This is valuable practice for your conscious mind to leave the mind-body connection alone!

With practice, this type of short meditation can refresh both your mind and body and you will be able to do it anywhere. It works well as a mid-day break at work or to relieve stress while traveling.

A few key thoughts about meditation…

Awareness. Any activity or task done with awareness is meditation. The act of meditating should make you aware of actions, thoughts and emotions. It is not concerned with the activity or the outcome. A present-moment state cannot have a judgment or a result.

Concentration. Concentration strengthens and works the mind. It creates a focus point. Meditation is the exact opposite. Meditation seeks to disconnect the mind. It loosens the hold your conscious mind has on thoughts and emotions. With meditation you should be relaxed and aware of everything not focused and intent.

Practice. Meditation can be done anywhere and can be practiced for a few moments or an hour. It is a tool not a goal or a result. Many meditation experts find that as meditation becomes part of their life, it blends into life with very little effort.

A mind stretched by a new experience can
never go back to its old dimension.
~ Oliver Wendell Holmes

Create a Centering Trigger

Having your mind in the present moment is a powerful tool but you must be able to get it there without a five-minute mediation session! Even two or three minutes is too long while you are getting ready for your class at a trial or test. Between warming up, keeping your dog's attention, and answering questions from the stewards or ring crew, two minutes of down time is a rarity. And, even if you get the time, a quiet spot for meditation might be hard to find ringside.

Thankfully, your conscious mind and body have a built in system that we can manipulate to instantly access a centered state. We can create a *mental trigger* for a calm, quiet mind. Your mind and body are already programmed to use mental triggers to communicate. "Triggers" are emotional or physiological responses to external stimuli. Smells, sounds, and touches are all very good mental triggers. For example, some common triggers.....

Sounds:
Car horn = alarm
Applause = success/happiness
Dog whine = concern

Smells:
Baby powder = cuddle
Coffee = wake-up
Smoke = alarm

Actions
High five = excitement
Tapping pen = focus
Prayer hands (palms together) = calm

Although these are common triggers, in reality, every individual has a different response to any given trigger. For example, a stage actor has a much stronger reaction to applause than a policeman. Anyone who's survived a house fire probably has a strong reaction to the smell of smoke. Those of us who are night owls can smell coffee in our sleep!

Live life to the fullest, and focus on the positive.
~Matt Cameron

Furthermore, triggers frequently get set up without us being consciously aware of them. Smells, sounds and touches are strong anchors for emotions and our minds are wired to constantly look for these associations. Sometimes these associations are positive. Having swum competitively into college, I still have a strong calming reaction to the smell of chlorine. On the flip side, some associations are negative or stressful. Kathleen has a harsh alarm/anxiety reaction to anyone grabbing both shoulders. I gave her the terrible news about the death of one of her dog's while I was holding her shoulders and a strong, negative association was built immediately.

We all live with these mental triggers and their associated memories, which subsequently generate an emotional response. Sometimes we are aware of them, sometimes not. For competitions, we want to hi-jack this system and deliberately setup a mental trigger for a calm, quiet mind. In order to do this, you need to build an association between a simple physical action or touch and a calm, present moment state. Once created your personal centering trigger will move your conscious mind into a calm, quiet state easily and almost instantly.

The process for creating a centering trigger is simple. When you have a calm-centered mind, simply add a predetermined touch or brief physical behavior. The touch or behavior will then be anchored to a calm-centered state of mind. A strong trigger can be setup in just a few sessions.

There are three easy steps to setting up a centering (calming) trigger.

1 - Select a touch.
2 - Settle your mind into a calm state using the 5-count breath exercise.
3 - Attach the touch behavior.

Select a touch. The first step is to select a simple physical action or touch as the anchor for your centering trigger. Although smells and sounds also work, it is easiest in a trial environment to use a touch or motion.

Select a touch that is simple and one action. It should be a specific motion/action that you do not regularly do. For example, rubbing your eyes or nose is a fairly common action. This does not make a good anchor since you frequently do it without conscious thought. The same goes for scratching motions. Your touch should be specific, brief and repeatable. Also avoid physical actions associated with stress, such as jaw clenching, a tight fist, or eye squeeze.

In addition, the action/motion should be self-contained to you. Do not select a touch that involves another person (high five or fist bump) or your dog (head pat, nose kisses or paw shake). Even though your friend and certainly your dog may be with you at the trial, it still makes you dependent on someone else to be calm.

Suggested touches or brief behaviors....

+ finger circle (thumb to index finger touch)
+ hand rub on thigh
+ gently closed fist
+ earlobe tug
+ back of neck squeeze
+ fist to forehead (i.e., Tebowing)
+ nose pinch
+ hair twirl

Nothing contributes so much to tranquilize
the mind as a steady purpose – a point
on which the soul can focus its intellectual eye.
~ Mary Shelley

Settle your mind into a calm, quiet state. A centering trigger uses your mind's instinctive process to link a physical stimulus to an emotion or an emotion to a stimulus. The process works both ways.

In order to link your selected touch with calm, you must first have a quiet mind. As you've already learned, the simplest way to quiet your thoughts and emotions is to move your body into a calm state. For this process, we use another breathing exercise.

Breath counting is a simple drill. It combines both a breathing drill and a mental focus exercise. It is an excellent way to establish a calm, quiet mind.

Exercise Steps

1 - Sit in a comfortable chair. Gently close your eyes and take a few deep breaths. Breathe naturally without trying to influence the depth or duration of your breaths. Let your hands rest comfortably in your lap.

2 - Count each exhale. Count "one" to yourself as you exhale. Next time count "two" and so on up to "five." This is one cycle.

3 - Begin a new cycle by starting over with "one" for the next exhale. Maintain this pattern for five cycles. Be aware of your body and any release of tension.

This is also an excellent exercise in which to add aromatherapy. Select a calming scent to enhance this breathing drill.

Attach the touch behavior. As you count through the five cycles of the breath counting exercise, be aware of your body. As your muscles relax, you may find yourself taking one or two deep breaths. The tension will leave your shoulders and neck. You may yawn or feel the need to stretch. All of these are signals that your body is connecting with your mind. You are moving into the present-state. As this happens, gently add your touch. Hold the position (e.g., finger circle) or slowly repeat the action (e.g., neck squeeze or thigh rub) for whatever remains of the five cycles. This is frequently referred to as loading your trigger.

A word of caution - triggers get worn out and reset. If you continuously use your centering trigger in a stressful environment, it may actually get set to trigger anxiety! Be aware of how your action/touch makes you feel. If it does not instantly generate a feeling of calm, you need to reset it. Take time to reload your centering trigger at regular intervals. If your trigger becomes strongly linked to stress, select and attach a different touch for calm.

If you focus on results, you will never change.
If you focus on change, you will get results
~unknown

Create a Key Phrase

If you are conscious, your mind is aware of something. It cannot be "blank." This rule applies even in the present moment. Your conscious mind must have something to do. Controlling your conscious mind enough to remain in a present-focus state requires that you structure its existence. This is the purpose behind simple counting drills, word games and meditation exercises. They give your conscious mind something to do while in the present moment. Mind games and meditation exercises are difficult to do in a competition environment. However, we also don't want to let your mind select what to focus on. You need to give it a focus point.

A focus point or phrase is often referred to as a "key phrase."

We particularly like the term key phrase since you are literally using a key thought to lock your conscious mind's attention on one action or purpose. In the sports world, this concept was adopted long ago by golfers. Almost all golf instructors and golf instruction manuals, talk about swing thoughts. The concept being that a swing thought is the thought the golfer holds in his mind immediately before or while swinging the club. For example, some common swing thoughts are "flexible knees," "body before arms," "low and slow," or "aim through the ball." These are just a few. There are as many swing thoughts as there are golfers.

Swing thought or key phrase theory translates easily into obedience, agility, herding and any other canine sport. We encourage our students to select a short, repeatable phrase. Short makes it easy for the conscious mind to repeat. A well chosen key phrase keeps your conscious mind busy with a positive, action oriented thought. For ourselves and our students, we have used all of the following…

- Eyes on dog's eyes.
- Heel toe. Heel toe.
- Short, quick steps.
- Elbows in.
- Work every foot.
- Quiet hands. Soft voice.
- Smile! This is the fun part.
- Whisper.
- Breathe deep and long.
- Brake. Plant. Stop.

- Lose, soft shoulders.
- Plant. Connect. Release.
- Direct with the hand.

Focus on remedies, not faults.
~ Jack Nicklaus

Some critical points about selecting your own key phrase....

Use active verbs. Your conscious mind can use words and images but your subconscious is limited to images. It is interesting to note that your conscious mind thinks first in pictures. Answer the following....

What animal produces milk?

What breed of dog is Scooby Doo?

What colors are on the American flag?

For each of the above questions, your mind produced an image first and then a word or words. You saw a cow, a goofy looking Great Dane, and an American flag as your mind selected the correct words. In order to tap into the simplicity of the image-word link for your key phrase, you want to select active verbs. For example, "Eyes on dog's eyes," is much more powerful than "Watch your dog." Active verbs engage both the conscious and subconscious mind.

Short and to the point. A key phrase should be easy to remember and easy to repeat. Saying, "I will keep my elbows at my side as I heel through the Figure 8." is way too long. A much better key phrase is simply, "Elbows in!" It should also be as short as possible. Saying, "Talk softly and quietly," is okay." Saying, "Whisper," is more effective.

One per course or exercise. Once you use your centering touch to move your mind into a calm state, you want to get it focused on task. To this end, you only want one key phrase. Juggling through your memory for the correct key phrase for an obstacle or an exercise is counterproductive. Particularly in agility, you should only use one key phrase, though you may have one for each type of course: standard, jumpers, snooker, gamblers, etc. In obedience or herding, which are considerably longer, you might want one or two; three at the absolute most. For example, on the out run portion of a test, you might use, "Whisper!" to keep your whistles or voice signals calm while your dog does the fetch. As you move into the drive portion, you may want to use, "Stand tall" to maintain a calm body posture. In a Utility test, you may use, "Elbows in" for heeling and signals but switch to "Mark it slow" for the glove retrieve and directed jumping.

Vary over time. Your key phrase is a focus point for your conscious mind. As such, it will change over time. As your handling, training, and mental management skills improve, your focus point will naturally change. Your key phrase should not change day-to-day.

Become more specific. As your mental focus improves and your ability to stay in the present during competitive events improves, your key phrase can become more specific. For example, we often counsel students to keep "Eyes on dog" while running a course. As the student's proficiency at this increases, the key phrase changes to "Eyes on dog's head" and then eventually to "Eyes on dog's eyes." This progression takes quite a few miles of course running!

Must be positive. As discussed previously, your conscious mind can grasp the concept of *no or not* but your subconscious mind has no such ability. If I tell you to *not* do something, your conscious mind understands but your subconscious misses the critical, negative point. Recall the example instruction: "Do not think about a lemon!" Your mind pictures a lemon even though the exercise was to *not* think of a lemon. This also applies to key phrases. Saying, "Don't shout" means half your mind is thinking about shouting! Change this key phrase to "Whisper," and you have a positive phrase that both conscious and subconscious mind can work on.

As knowledge increases, wonder deepens.
~ Charles Morgan

Write it down. Create a key phrase or phrases for your next competition. Work with your coach or training partner to find a focus point that works for your competitive situation. Everyone will have a different key phrase. The key phrase should focus on a training issue or handling movement and should steady and calm your mind. Once you've worked out your key phrase or phrases, write them down. Make sure they are comfortable and easy to repeat.

Nikki – Focused and calm

#3
Clear
Focus

A calm, centered mind is actually a bit dangerous. Your conscious mind is now free to focus solely on one thing with great intensity. This is an awesome power! It must, however, be used with care.

There are two ways to focus your mind. You can focus on success or on failure. Our job is to give you the tools to be absolutely certain that your mind locks onto success. It is easy to obsess about all the ways you can fail, particularly when success is narrowly defined like "Win Nationals." In about one hour, I could knock out a seriously long list on the ways you can NOT win Nationals. Even for naturally optimistic people, it can be hard to fixate on success when faced with a big task.

Fortunately, with a calm, centered mind, you can easily learn to avoid or minimize the negatives and achieve your dream.

Obstacles are those frightening things you see
when you take your eyes off the goal.
~Hanah More

In order to be successful, you must know exactly what it is you want to accomplish. So, the first order of business is to be sure your final goal is clearly defined. For example, one of our students got a Top Five ranking for her breed and received an invitation to the AKC Agility Invitational. Nice! Right? Sure, she was happy about the Agility Invitational but it was not her definition of success. She and her dog got somewhere significant but it wasn't where she was aiming! With double Q's a rare commodity for them, success to her was defined as a MACH.

Getting to where you want to go requires a plan; otherwise known as a defined goal. Goal setting is a skill set that is learned through basic trial and error. There are plenty of business and sports psychology books written on effective goal setting. Some methods are complex, involving specialized software, and some are as simple as an enlarged to-do list. Of course, there are pros and cons to every method. Whatever approach you decide on, you must invest a bit of time and give it some serious thought. Goal planning is absolutely necessary to maintain focus. Without a definite destination, you won't know where you'll end up. It might be someplace wonderful but it can just as easily be a waste of time and effort.

One of the easiest techniques for successful goal setting is to divide and conquer. Goal planning should not be so arduous that you avoid it like income taxes! So, with all of our students, we break the concept of a goal into three distinct components:

- Dream

- Journey

- Baby Steps

You must begin with a dream. You can then layout the journey that will make that dream real. And then you must identify the baby steps – the nitty-gritty, little details - that make it all happen. Although sometimes a bit tedious, the goal setting and tending process gives your conscious mind something tangible to focus on and keeps it focused on success.

When you begin this process, keep in mind the timeframes within the dream, journey and baby steps phases. As you dream, let your imagination go forward a year or two or three. What can you accomplish if you worked on it for a thousand days? Think in terms of years when you dream. When you contemplate the path (the journey) to achieving your dream, you will want to think in terms of months. Goals need to be managed and revised as you make progress so a three to six month plan works best. And, finally, when you drill down to the specific steps, you should be thinking a week or a day. This is where the action is. In the baby steps, you target specific tasks that need to be finished for forward progress. Decide what you will accomplish in a training session, learn from a seminar, or what benefit should be obtained from an on-line class.

Correctly laid out goal plans also allow you to use periodization training. Periodization techniques organize all your training goals and needs into logical segments with different focus points and specific timeframes for each piece. For example, heading into the 2014 AKC Agility Nationals, we created an eighteen week goal plan for one of our students. It consisted of three six-week periods. The first six-week segment focused on fitness. The second was structured around skill development and foundation training and the third was built on full course work. Athletes who use periodization training fully understand that improvement happens in cycles (i.e., not linear) and that the cycle of improvement/success can be under their control. It also seriously reduces the possibility of over training and aims to peak your dog at a specific point in time. A periodization plan also balances time, resources and effort so you can relax and enjoy the process!

> Dreams come true; without that possibility nature would not incite us to have them.
> ~John Updike

Our thoughts create our reality – where we put our
focus is the direction we tend to go.
~Peter McWilliams

Dream

Your first job is to spend time dreaming. Do it big and bold! Many people have a dream, a plan for the future that excites them. These fortunate folks are already motivated and enthused with energy. If you don't yet have a big, fantastic dream, let your imagination go wild. Enjoy a few daydreams. What do you find thrilling? What makes you want to grin at a wall or dance across the kitchen? If you have trouble really letting your imagination go into uncharted territory, try buying a lottery ticket. Hold the ticket in your hands and imagine having millions of dollars. What would you do? Where would you go? What new ideas occur to you?

Pick a dream that inspires you and makes you feel alive, passionate and energized. It should also be a little bit scary.

For those of you with highly developed imaginations, who have or can easily find multiple dreams, pick one. You can have it all but you can only have it one piece at a time. Sort through your dreams and select the one that most excites you.

As you begin to live your dream, keep the following in mind…

Dream your own dream. Dog sports are played at multiple levels and each of you is free to decide at what level (local, national, international, etc) you want to play. And, every individual should decide at what intensity they want to compete. Some of our students come to us specifically to leverage off our international experience. They want to train and compete for spots on the USA teams for FCI World Championships, the IFCI World Championships, or the European Open. Representing the USA at one of the world championship events is an excellent dream. Others come to us with a dream to qualify for the Invitational or to finish a MACH. Some just want to put letters after their dogs' names. Others join an agility class to have fun with their dog and get some exercise. All – and everything in between – are excellent dreams. You decide what you want.

Eliminate all limits. Dream without constraints or limits. Let your imagination fly free without boundaries. It is okay to recognize that there will be challenges and a few risks but a solution can be found. You must trust that within the goal-setting process you will figure out how to provide the money, time and resources necessary. This is the best part of a lottery-winning dream. Having unlimited funds makes many other limits disappear! Removing limitations, barriers, and the "that's not possible" thoughts from your mind is a necessary leap of faith. Believe that anything is possible and that somehow things will just – more or less magically - work out in your favor when it is supposed to.

World Team Tryouts 2010

At the beginning of 2010, Demon was not on a short list for the AKC World Team. There were five or six excellent dogs with much better chances for making team. If I had looked at the competition and given up, Demon would not have been on the 2010 team. I had blind faith that if I just worked my mental management issues, trained Demon to improve his speed and skills, and stayed positive, my dream would come true. If not in 2010, then the next year or the next (730 days is a long time!). Fortunately, for Demon and I, the situation changed rather dramatically.

In 2010, the World Championships were in Germany at a horse arena so the world team coaches moved the USA tryouts from the Hopkins Arena, which is turf, to the University of Minnesota's horse arena, which is dirt. They wanted to see the dogs compete on a dirt surface since it changes how the dogs run and jump.

Demon loves dirt! Running on his favorite surface and in excellent physical condition, he was faster and tighter than in previous years. We had also trained hard all winter. None of the handling challenges were a surprise. Furthermore, using my new mental management skills to focus on my dog and on my routines, I was able to completely ignore the arena conditions, which were less than ideal. It was a freezing cold, wet weekend spent in an unheated dirt barn. With trust in the process, I went into tryouts against the odds and gave Demon his chance. He won his spot on Sunday. It was a fantastic Mother's Day present!

Put it in writing. Dreams are elusive and wispy until you write them down. Once on paper they immediately exist. They become concrete and all too real. When they're put in writing, dreams take shape and gain substance. It's simple…type or write down your dream. You need to be able to look at it and work a plan around it. Just saying, "I want to earn an OTCH," is not enough. Pick up a pen and write it down. The dream will instantly become very real. Writing or typing your dream every week or day also makes it less scary and more achievable every time you write it.

Let your dream surround you. It is also wonderful if you can surround yourself with images and real pictures of your dream. Put them on your office wall or use them as your screensaver on your computer and phone. Images that make your dream real will keep it in focus and make it your reality. For example, I started using red, white and blue for Demon's colors. Seeing his leash, blankets, and coats with USA colors and the American flag was a constant, positive reminder of my dream of one day representing the USA in international competition.

We have students who use inspirational phrases and photos as their screensavers. Others surround themselves with subtle reminders of where they want to go like drinking their morning coffee from mug with a picture of the city hosting Nationals or wearing tee-shirts with motivational, stick-with-it phrases or having a corkboard or bulletin board plastered with ribbons, notes, photos and mementoes of their best competition days.

If it's a big competition you want to compete at, put the dates in your calendar and let it be part of your planning. Make it real!

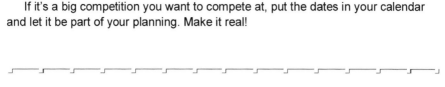

Put Your Head in the Clouds

Stick your head up in the clouds and take a look around at everything that could be. Strangely, everyone always says that being stuck in the clouds is wrong so you fall back to earth. Welcome to reality! But is it? Reality doesn't have to be absolute. Your reality depends solely on what you make of it. The "realistic" goals others set for you will always fall just short of the fairy tale version of Cloud 9 in your mind. Personally, I don't mind living with my head in the clouds, sure everything gets foggy every now and then, and it is awfully bright but then again the future is too.

The reality people keep ranting about is entirely based around problems. Think about it, no one ever welcomes you to reality when something good happens. Reality is entirely negative. It is obstacles and statistics and all the things standing in your way wrapped up in one neat little bundle. Recognizing that, why anyone would want to be realistic is beyond me. For me, reality will always seem like an illusion, a trick, that other people fool you into believing. It keeps you firmly on the ground with no way of shooting for the stars or taking a leap of faith. You can't even pop your head into the clouds to imagine "What-if?" Reality should give you wings, like red-bull only without all the caffeine.

Agility & Beyond Blog - Kathleen Oswald - June 18, 2013

Short and sweet is best. Your dream should be simple and concrete. When you write your dream, keep it short and very specific. For example, typing, "I want to compete well enough to earn an agility championship," is not as powerful as putting, "I want a MACH," in writing. Both statements have the same basic goal – to become a better handler to earn MACH points and double Q's – but the second is sharp and specific.

No timeframe. The very best dreams are big and require considerable effort. To this end, they should not have time constraints. For example, "Win the 2013 AKC Obedience Invitational," is a very time specific dream. Writing "Win the AKC Obedience Invitational" is equally valid and allows you to work hard without a strict timeframe. Dreams without time constraints allow for life, injuries and the unexpected. The same dream without a deadline can keep you from losing focus when life throws you a curve.

Live backward. Sometimes life gives us Eureka! moments. I read the following quote in *Extraordinary Golf* by Fred Shoemaker and it immediately changed the way I lived my life.

Extraordinary people live their lives backward.
They create a future and live into it.

Our mind puts a filter on everything so events have meaning and actions have purpose. When you alter that filter, you completely change how you live.

Think about this...if you were the current national champion, how would you train, plan, workout, trial, budget, etc? What would be different? Most competitors obsess about what needs to be fixed or retrained or added to achieve success and often lose sight of what they already have. Striving for success creates doubt and stress. However, we all live in the world through our perceptions. If you can change your perspective to the future, where you have already achieved your dream, then many decisions become easier. Distractions and disruptions fade faster. And, worries and fears dissolve in happy memories. Here's the secret that Fred Shoemaker was sharing, you don't actually have to win a national championship to live as if you have!

Journey

Once you have a dream, you need to plot a pathway into the future where your dream is reality. Knowing where you want to go is only the first part of the process. The next step requires some serious thought and attention to detail. A rewarding journey requires well thought out goals.

Lots of people have dreams and many layout goals. Unfortunately, the result isn't always success. Identifying the components of your journey - the actual goals - requires creativity, attention to detail, and practice. The most difficult part is determining what pieces to focus on. Again, for ourselves and our students, we divide the task into pieces in order to gain control over the process.

There are two types of goals: performance goals and personal goals. Your journey must incorporate both.

Performance goals. These are the goals that challenge you and/or your dog's skills and abilities. They relate directly to how well you compete with your dog. Most of these will be accomplished in training or prepping for competition. These goals should be specific and measureable. Some examples are...

- Improve heeling accuracy in the Figure 8 exercise.
- Increase height of open field disc toss.
- Sharpen dog's focus and attention on start line.
- Lengthen outrun.
- Improve accuracy and speed of weave poles performance.
- Increase speed of A-frame performance.

Every sport and every level of training will have unique performance goals. If you are not sure, spend some time with your coach or instructor to determine what your current performance goals should be. We frequently have mini-goal planning sessions with our students during down time at trials or over the phone. We identify short and long range performance goals for them to use during the goal planning steps.

Personal goals. On the other side are personal goals. These are the goals that *you* need to accomplish. Personal goals range from increased physical fitness to improved mental management skills to budgeting to travel plans. Most of these goals will be accomplished away from the training/trialing environment. Some examples are...

* Save enough money to fly to USDAA Agility Nationals.
* Improve my goal setting abilities.
* Join a fitness class to improve my running speed.
* Organize my trial notes and videos to improve feedback information.
* Plan a road trip to your breed's nationals in St. Louis, MO.

You must work on both performance and personal goals. They complement each other and give you options for working on your dream wherever you are or whenever time allows. For example, we have several students who frequently get sent out of town on business. It's always last minute and can seriously disrupt their training plans for their dogs. Although their performance goals have to go on hold for a day

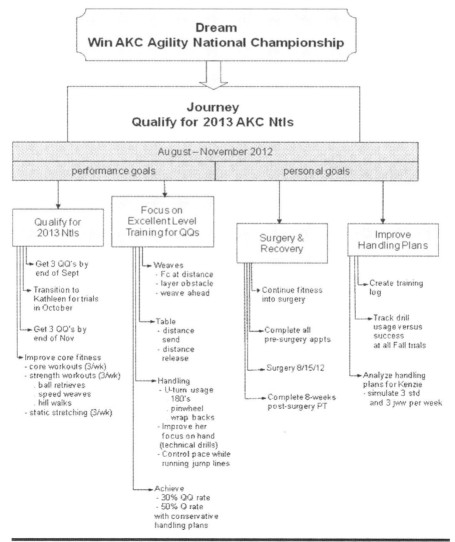

or two, their personal goals do not. We encourage them to download their trial videos onto their laptops and do some serious analysis on their past performances and training sessions. Video analysis is time consuming but it's a perfect activity (sound off!) for time in flight or an evening spent at a hotel. They can also use the extra away or travel time to evaluate and review their goal plans. What has been accomplished? What should be added or changes? Travel time is also a great time to catch up on reading, blogging or designing new training sets. Alternately, when a snowstorm or hurricane forces a trial to cancel and you have a three-day weekend wide open, you can work on all your performance skills for thirty-six hours. Think about how many short training sessions you can build into these newly found days. We have more than one student who has turned their living room into a jump course.

The point is...when you identify both performance and personal goals, you can continue to work on your dream no matter where you are or what the circumstances.

> *Performance and personal goals complement each other and give you options for working on your dream wherever you are or whenever time allows.*

With a focus on the future versus groaning about an unexpected business trip or lousy weather, you can be productive and busy. Often when our routines or plans are disrupted, it just takes time to get mentally reorganized. With a goal plan, you have the perfect tool to shift your focus and move onto a new task.

When you are laying out the details of your journey, keep in mind the following guidelines for setting goals.

Set goals that support your dream. Every goal should directly affect your dream. In any given month, there are millions of ways to spend your time and dollars. When you are living your dream, you need to align those resources and your efforts to the goals that move you closer to your dream. For example, when Betsy Scapicchio, one of the top USA obedience competitors and instructors, is focused on getting a dog qualified for AKC National Obedience Championships or the Invitational, she doesn't start herding lessons. Sure sheep herding is fun, but it also introduces different physical demands on her border collie and it drains resources (time and money). Cross-training and conditioning with herding might be valuable but not until she is in a non-competition phase.

Two other common problems that you should guard against are: scope explosion and tangents.

Scope explosion. This is a common problem in project management. Scope explosion refers to the "explosion" of a well laid out project with additional goals and required outcomes. For example, one of our students dreamed for years about making the Finals at a national event with her dog and in 2013 we built a plan – with all the performance and personal goals well defined - to get her there. About two months before the event, I found her obsessing in training about her dog's yards-per-second. Since this wasn't a part of the current goal plan, I started digging and quickly discovered that she was really dreaming about that top spot on the podium. The difference between making Finals and winning was significant for this team. She expanded her dream! A win at nationals might be very doable in the future but making Finals and winning required very different goals.

Tangents. Also watch out for tangents. If you happen to be in a car commercial for Land Rover, then random turns to nowhere or an unplanned side trip are cool and adventuresome. When you are laying out a goal plan, detours and side trips sap resources and add complications. They are deadly for accomplishing your goals. For instance, one of the most difficult parts of competing at a national level is the desire to also travel for fun. Why go all the way to Florida in December and see nothing? This is really hard to explain to your co-workers in the office! You spent seven days in sunny Florida and only saw the inside of a convention center? Sightseeing trips (aka side trips and detours), should be carefully balanced with the goal of competing successfully. Walking for two or three hours along the beach may not help your dog prepare for the weekend event. The photo of your pup chasing sea gulls through the surf makes a fabulous Facebook post but at what cost? Plan your trip carefully so your focus is on the event. You can incorporate vacation time into your trip, just be sure detours do not cause conflicts with your goals or sap resources!

The will to succeed is important, but what's more important is the will to prepare.
~ Bobby Knight

It's Who You Are

It's never the glory. It's never the score. It's not about seeing who's less or who's more. Cause when you find out how fast and how far, you'll know it's not how much you have. It's who you are.
The Climb by Miley Cyrus.

Dog training isn't about climbing to the top. It isn't about winning. The journey we take with our dogs isn't about the sport. It is about the process. While many of our goals are physical, tangible experiences, much of our successes happen within us and between us and our dog. Whether we realized it or not, each experience, each show, each run or test or trial, and even each dog we encounter, offers us new material to learn from. The lessons we take from our greatest successes and our most heart-breaking failures, mold who we are and who we will become in the future. No dream is out of reach. We simply have to be brave enough to reach for it. For a journey isn't about getting somewhere. It's about becoming someone you want to be. Have a dream so big you can never achieve it and then be the person who can.

Agility and Beyond Blog - Kathleen Oswald - May 7, 2013

Goals must be process-oriented. Individual goals should focus on the process – the journey – not just the end result. Focus your thoughts and efforts on the actual actions needed to attain your goals. It is more effective than fixating on the dream – the result.

As you learn to use goals to achieve your dreams, you may find that the journey is as satisfying (or perhaps more so) than reaching your dream. Winning a spot on the AKC World Team was fantastic but learning to run Demon on tough international-style courses was a daily thrill, especially since Kathleen was there with me through every step. The journey was a dream in its own right.

Goals must be specific. Consider the difference between "Run faster," and "Run forty yards in six seconds." The first is actually rather vague. How is faster defined? How will you know if you accomplish the goal?

Every goal must be measurable in some way. For example, if your goal is to have enough money to fly to California for the AKC Obedience Invitational, you must first know how much money you will need. What does it actually cost to fly yourself and your dog to California and stay there for a week? Will you need five hundred, one thousand or three thousand dollars? For most people, there is a big difference between five hundred and three thousand dollars! With a little bit of work on the Internet or with a travel agent, you can get a valid estimate. With this amount, you can then create a savings plan and can measure each month whether you are saving enough.

> *When you are living your dream, you must align your resources and efforts to the goals that move you closer to the dream. Other activities – for yourself or your dog - should be evaluated and considered very carefully.*

This same rule applies to your dog's performance. We frequently have students tell us their dogs' weaves are too slow. Translating this into a wish for faster weave poles, the first question is always, "How many seconds does it take him to complete the weaves?" More often than not the student does not know the answer to this question. Getting out the video camera or the stopwatch is almost always the first step. We cannot get "faster" weaves without actually knowing what the dog's current time is and then setting a goal time. Without a starting point, we cannot measure our progress or know when we're successful.

Goals must be attainable It is also important that the goal be attainable. If you decide that running "faster" means covering forty yards in 4.25 seconds, then you should dump dog sports and sign-up for the NFL. The fastest NFL sprinters cover forty yards in that time! A much better plan is to actually time yourself running forty yards. You now have a benchmark. You have a concrete time that you can now work to beat.

Apply this concrete-and-real rule to every goal: performance and personal. Ask yourself if you can accomplish the goal (real) and how you will know when you do (concrete). This makes sure all your goals are attainable.

Applying this rule to your goals does not mean that the goal must be easy - perhaps you really do want to run forty yards in under five seconds! It just has to be measureable and doable.

I compete to challenge myself not the
competition.
~Kathleen Oswald

Every goal should be under your control. Consider a goal like, "Win the Utility B class at the Western Pennsylvania Dog Show." It is short and specific and doable. However, at any given event, you do not control who wins. By definition, it is a competition so there are other athletes competing directly against you. Your very best effort that day or weekend may not win the Utility class. You cannot control the efforts of your competitors or the scoring whims of the judge. You can only do your very best and enjoy your own success.

A much better goal is "Win a Utility B class," which eliminates the control issue of a specific event or "I want to be a competitive force at the WPD show," which sets your sights on your own success. You get to decide whether you were competitive. Think about the day when you and your dog achieve your first 199 ½ in Open B. Shouldn't your trip home be like flying through the clouds? What a fabulous effort your dog gave if the judge could only deduct half a point from the entire test. What if that 199 ½ was beat by someone that day who scored a 200? Do you really want to let someone else's results diminish your pup's wonderful day?

I don't focus on what I'm up against.
I focus on my goals and I try to ignore the rest.
~Venus Williams

Goals have timeframes not deadlines. Setting a specific deadline is occasionally necessary, like when you are publishing a book! However, a drop-dead date attached to a goal adds considerable stress. Goals are much better setup without restricting timeframes. Some goals are achieved quickly; others take awhile to achieve. Give yourself and your dog the freedom to develop and evolve. You'll both enjoy the journey more.

When working on performance and personal goals, think in terms of three to six months. What can you accomplish in one hundred and twenty days? Several months is enough time to keep the result real so you stay motivated. A goal that requires six-months - like change jobs so you have more training time - is fine so long as you do not add pressure with a deadline set in concrete.

Goals should be managed and revised. Every goal should be consistently evaluated. Revisions to your goal plan are a fundamental part of the process. After you complete a goal or set of tasks within a goal, you need to modify the goal to continue the process of improving.

For example, when Kathleen first took Jenna to World Team Tryouts, Jenna was still inconsistent with her dog walk and A-frame performances. So, for the summer and fall, a large part of her skill level exercises focused on zone work. Contact drills became a large part of Jenna's training sessions and Kathleen had to be very creative with her drills. Creating performance errors on the contacts in practice can be very difficult. By their second trip to Tryouts, Kathleen's confidence in her ability to hit the zone was much higher. With this part of their journey completed, Kathleen was able to revise her goal plan to focus on more speed and more lateral distance, which gave them valuable flexibility in handling.

Some goals – like the need to retrain Jenna's dog walk – take time. Other goals are realized quickly, like teaching her to jump the backside of a wing jump. Both Demon and Jenna learned this skill in a weekend. Kathleen and I were able almost immediately to revise our goal plans to include another task. Revisions and adjustments are all part of managing your journey.

Balance goals with available resources. Dream without limits but you must set goals, which have much shorter timeframes, within the boundaries of your available resources. When you decide what goals to setup for the near future, consider how much time, money and effort you will have and need. Be realistic with your estimates. Working within your goal plan should help you make sharp, clear choices.

For example, one of our students with a very fast terrier proposed entering twelve agility trials in one month (which is possible twice a year in New Jersey) to collect points for the Agility Invitational. Although the plan sounded great, when we laid out the schedule, the time and money required for that many trials in one month did not realistically fit within her budget or work schedule. We went back to the event calendar and added several big cluster shows on the East Coast earlier in the fall. She ended up with the same number of trials with less time off work and fewer nights on the road. On the other hand, we did use the overloaded New Jersey trial schedule to qualify one student for the AKC Nationals. Margaret had a very consistent, mature dog with all its double Qs but she was out with an injury for the summer. She came back in the fall but needed quite a few points. Margaret was able to find a travel buddy with the same trial schedule and joining forces with a friend to share costs worked out great for her and her dog!

Resource allocation is a personal choice. The idea is to balance your available resources with your goals. It's easy to find creative solutions to problems when you know what the issue is!

Goals must be written down. By writing or typing your goals, you make them real and make it possible to track your progress. It is almost impossible to keep an entire goal plan in your head. Putting goals on paper also allows you to review your progress, which builds confidence and keeps you focused. It also makes the process easier the next time. With a detailed written goal plan, your knowledge and efforts can be recycled.

Goals are planned. There is a huge difference between a set of goals and a wish. A goal is defined as the result attained when effort is directed at it. A goal is an objective that is planned and prepared for. It has purpose within a bigger plan that is detailed and well documented. Some of our students used to set "goals" for a weekend or large tournament but they don't actually prepare or setup a plan to achieve their purpose. This is the definition of a want or wish. It is not goal setting as we define it.

Do or do not. There is no try.
~Yoda

A few last thoughts on goals....setup performance and personal goals that require some serious work but your goals should not look like a weekend to-do list. Your goal chart should be exciting and interesting. It should inspire you every time you set eyes on it. If you are new to goal setting, then you are building a new skill. It will not be a perfect process and there are no guarantees. It may take several attempts and some serious effort and time for you to realize your dream.

As you learn to setup and use goal planning, what you accomplish is sometimes an intangible. Learning to think positive and have confidence in oneself are definite side benefits to goal planning. You will also be learning the habits that underlay every high performance team. Winning habits – like successful goal planning – can be applied to everything you do in life from dog sports to your career to buying a house to planning for retirement. This is a valuable skill well worth the time it takes to develop it.

The progress and improvement built into goal plans are the paving stones to your dream and each stone is very small when compared to the entire journey!

Strong foundations are needed
to build castles.
~Jerry Lynch

Baby Steps

Once a set of goals is laid out, you must identify the actions needed to achieve the objectives within the plan. These are the actual jobs that get the goal finished. The real nitty-gritty stuff is at this level. This is also where timeframes are appropriate and very important.

Baby steps are the actions that you do each week and day. The steps under each goal must be doable, interesting and specific. Every task should be something you can do. There is no way to make this easy but it is fairly simple. You have to sit down, read each goal and identify what actions, tasks, jobs, etc are needed to achieve that goal. The phrase "Just Do It" often applies. You may need to do some investigating or talk to your trainer, coach, physical therapist or other professional to expand your knowledge of what is required. You may need that stopwatch! With a working goal plan, the steps can be laid out over the course of a few weeks. You don't have to design three months of tasks in one brain draining session.

Keep the following in mind as you layout the tasks beneath each goal...

Each task must be specific. These are the actual steps that make the goal achievable. You need details. Mostly this is just grunt work. Make a list of actual tasks to be completed and then go do them.

During the summer of 2012, Kathleen set a goal for Whimzy to improve her speed over the seesaw from 2.2 seconds to 1.2 seconds. After some consideration, Kathleen created several seesaw drills and laid out a plan to work those drills three times per week. At the end of each month, she took video of Whimzy on the seesaw to measure her progress. Kathleen had a specific goal (shave one second off Whimzy's seesaw performance) and laid out specific tasks (seesaw drills done three times per week at three different facilities). The results were measureable and she was able to revise her tasks over the course of the three months.

Some other examples of specific tasks that our students have listed under their goals...

 * Train a rear-cross on the weave poles
 * Complete utility article training
 * Teach Figure 8 heeling pattern
 * Improve dog's core fitness
 * Improve dog's stamina with 12-15 miles of walks/hikes per week
 * Budget and schedule two physical therapy session per month for dog
 * Train consistent two jump lead-out from start line
 * Create and use a daily training log
 * Switch dog to raw diet
 * Improve dog's diet & health by baking all my own treats

Create a daily journal or log. Keeping track, of what you are doing and why, is a critical component to achieving your dream. The rewards far, far outweigh the time needed to maintain a daily log. The one shown on the right is what I use. It doesn't matter how you organize the information or where you keep it (binder or computer). There are multiple advantages to keeping a daily log.

First, you get to write down your dream. Writing (or typing) your dream on each week's entries makes it real. You will own that dream and it will be less scary as you make it part of who you are on a daily basis (live in your future).

Second, you must record your goals. Some goals are easy to achieve; others require quite a bit of effort and time. Writing them down not only lets you stay aware of them, it provides a plan of action. Life happens and everyone gets off track or distracted. Having a journey laid out on paper lets you get back to work quickly. Writing individual goals down also makes them part of your life. It is also important to classify each goal as performance or personal.

The third and final step is to record the specific tasks to be accomplished. This is the actual to-do list. Think about what you can do in a training session or over the course of a few days. Tasks then have timeframes and/or completion dates. It is this detailed record that creates confidence.

| 2012 Agility Training Log | | | Week _____ |

| Dream _____ |

Fitness & Conditioning	
Day	Activity
_____	_____
_____	_____
_____	_____
_____	_____
_____	_____
_____	_____
_____	_____
_____	_____
_____	_____
_____	_____
_____	_____

Strength Training	
Day	Activity
_____	_____
_____	_____
_____	_____
_____	_____
_____	_____
_____	_____

Nutrition/Meds/Notes

Miscellaneous

Training Specifics		
Day	Location	Focus/Activity
_____	_____	_____
_____	_____	_____
_____	_____	_____
_____	_____	_____
_____	_____	_____
_____	_____	_____
_____	_____	_____

Check progress on goals periodically. You should be referencing your task lists frequently to be sure you are on track. There is no point thinking your way through the whole process and then leave your plan sitting on your desk or buried in a folder on your computer. There shouldn't be any dust (real or metaphorical) on your goal plan!

Mark the tasks as you complete them or note the date range that you worked on each item. For example, with Kathleen's seesaw drills, she noted which day(s) each week that she did seesaw drills and also which drill. She also periodically took video of Whimzy completing the seesaw to record her progress, to look for differences in behavior, and to check that her time was improving. This consistent record keeping let Kathleen know that the drills were working and kept her motivated throughout the entire summer. As Whimzy quickly achieved the goal time of 1.2 seconds, Kathleen was also able to modify her goal plan to include some different handling moves – rear-cross and distance - around the seesaw.

Allow new habits to grow. Habits require approximately one hundred days to become part of your programming. Give yourself those crucial three months to ingrain the new habit. After three months, you can move onto new tasks and just periodically check that the new habit is still in place. This is one of the largest benefits of becoming task-oriented. It is very, very true that winning is habit. If a goal requires a specific behavior, you can ingrain that action into your life. Once there, you will find it much easier to maintain.

> If opportunity doesn't knock,
> build a door.
> ~Milton Bearle

Early in Demon's training career, I made a decision to modify his diet to include specific supplements, extra fat and a wider variety of proteins. The first few months required sticky notes everywhere as reminders to add this or cook that or buy more yogurt, pumpkin, salmon, pork, bison, etc. Today, I just sweep through the grocery store adding his special items to the cart without a thought and my husband and son even know which stuff is for Demon and don't eat it anymore!. It took awhile to develop a new shopping habit and then to expand the quantities as our household pack increased from three to five to seven dogs but now it's a solid, ingrained (slightly budget busting) behavior.

Make the tasks fun and interesting. Boredom has killed more goal plans than laziness. Your task list should not read and feel like a to-do list of household chores. Sometimes it's just plan hard work and pure gritty determination that gets you moving but not all the time. If every day feels like hard work, you may have the wrong dream or goal. Your tasks – particularly knowing that accomplishing each one gets you that much closer to your dream – should inspire and energize you! Sometimes though you just need to modify how you approach a set of tasks to improve the likelihood of doing them. When you are setting up your tasks, think more than a little bit about how you will accomplish them. Perhaps you would be more motivated and committed to bi-weekly training sessions if you had a training partner? A friend can help keep those training sessions firmly on the calendar. Perhaps you could do two classes each week rather than one? Having trouble saving money or sticking to a budget? Perhaps you should hire a financial planner? Getting expert advice is sometimes both indispensable and a major advantage.

After a series of small injuries and facing hip replacement surgery, one of my biggest personal goals in 2012 was to improve my fitness. For several years, I had laid out detailed workouts but my fitness level varied as did my commitment to exercising and stretching regularly. So, in order to accomplish my personal goal of improved fitness, I setup training sessions twice a week with a personal trainer. Although the cost is considerably higher than working out on my own, I now have set timeframes for workouts and I have an expert guiding me through those workouts. With my personal trainer's guidance,

> *Boredom kills more goal plans than laziness.*

I have not only improved my overall fitness but I no longer have to spend time setting up or laying out workouts and I have changed how I run to prevent further injuries.

So, as you build your to-do list, give serious thought to what will get you to actually do all the tasks. For most trainers, the easy part is working the dog but you must do much more than that for a successful goal plan! Look at your task list and think creatively. Sometimes you may even need to think outside the box!

Consider the following task plan that I discussed for one of my students in 2009. Margaret decided to drive her Rottweiler, Magnus, to the AKC Agility Invitational. She and her husband agreed to drive about ten hours per day, assumed twenty-four miles per gallon, and decided to depart on Saturday morning. With this, in less than fifteen seconds, the map software on her computer gave them the entire route for a five day trip plus provided thirteen refueling spots and four recommended overnight stops. This impressive feat of software engineering gave them a very doable trip.

<u>Margaret's Driving Plan</u>
Depart NYC
 - refuel Spring Run, PA
 - refuel Barnesville, PA
Overnight stop #1 in Springfield, OH
 - refuel Greens Fork, IN
 - refuel Altamont, IL
 - refuel Saint Robert, MO
Overnight stop #2 in Springfield, MO
 - refuel Adair, OK
 - refuel Hydro, OK
 - refuel Busland, TX
Overnight stop #3 in Adrian, TX
 - refuel Clines Corner, NM
 - refuel Houck, AZ
Overnight stop #4 in Rimrock, AZ
 - refuel Mayer, AZ
 - refuel Tacna, AZ
Arrive San Diego, CA

The map software gave them highway-to-highway directions through eleven states and dozens of big cities. Margaret considered her plan complete and the task done. I wasn't so convinced when we reviewed the details. Although the journey would be successful – they would leave New York and arrive in California – it was missing more than a little critical information.

A look at the problems within Margaret's plan illustrates how goal setting frequently goes awry.

First, we must do a simple reality check. Does the plan accomplish the goal? If you are planning to haul the contents of your house coast-to-coast in a U-haul truck, then yes. This plan is sufficient. If you are traveling thousands of miles with your dog on the way to a major tournament, then no this plan is not sufficient. While it does move two people and a dog from the east to west coast, it does not really meet the needs of the humans or of a performance dog like Magnus. The map software plan fails to incorporate the dog's need to potty/stretch, get serious exercise to maintain fitness, and have large, quiet hotel rooms to stretch out and relax.

> *Goal setting is about taking charge of those elements that you can control.*

A second major issue is boredom. The software planned trip is fine but generic and uninspiring. Faced with this trip plan on Saturday morning, most of us would be inclined to roll over and go back to sleep! Dreams require hard work but five days of straight driving is not a task. It's torture.

> Happiness is not something you postpone for the future; it is something you design for the present.
> ~John Rohn

So, how do we setup a plan that meets our goals and inspires us to actually do it? The answer is to be creative, do some investigating, and make it your personal. Consider this alternate plan.

Magnus's Excellent Cross-Country Adventure.
Depart NYC
- refuel Blue Mountain Service Plaza on I-78; the travel plaza has a Starbucks, Pizza Hut, DQ and large dog walk area
- refuel in Zanesville, OH and extend afternoon stop to include visit to Dillon State Park where Magnus can run along reservoir and play fetch in large fields

Overnight stop #1 in Dayton, OH
- Hotel reservation at Marriott Residence Inn with an indoor pool and close to The Greene, an outdoor shopping area with multiple restaurants and areas to wander with Magnus after dinner
- refuel in Cloverdale, IN and extend morning stop to include short hike along river near waterfalls in Cagles Mill State Park
- refuel in Saint Louis, MO and extend afternoon stop to include hike thru Gateway Arch Park with Magnus and tourist and photography stop for Margaret and her husband

Overnight stop #2 in Springfield, MO
- Hotel reservation at Courtyard by Marriott
- refuel in Tulsa, OK and extend morning stop to include a long walk for Magnus on ten miles of paved paths along Arkansas River in downtown area
- refuel anywhere on Route 66; vary trip with travel on Route 66 anywhere between Missouri and Oklahoma City to enjoy the tourist stops and photo opportunities for Margaret's husband

Overnight stop #3 in Amarillo, TX
- Hotel reservation at Staybridge Suites with indoor pool
- refuel in Albuquerque, NM and extend late morning stop to include a one to three mile hike at Petroglyph National Monument for Magnus to stretch and get exercise and take time for more photo opportunities

-refuel in Chambers, AZ and then stop later in the afternoon to visit the Petrified Forest National Park south of Chambers and Holbrook for more exercise time for Magnus

Overnight stop #4 in Holbrook, AZ
- Hotel reservation at Ramada Limited
- Refuel in Flagstaff, AZ and extend travel time to visit (1.5 hours north) to Grand Canyon National Park where dogs are allowed on leash on south rim visitor areas
- Refuel in Rimrock, AZ

Overnight stop #5 in Phoenix, AZ
- Stay overnight at brother's house in Glendale, AZ where there is a large fenced yard with a few pieces of agility equipment so Magnus can get some basic training and work his muscles doing agility
- refuel Coyote Wells, CA and extend stop to include short hikes in Anza-Borrego Desert State Park for Magnus to get exercise

Arrive Long Beach, CA

Compare the two cross-country trips. Which would you want to do? Which would you want to read about or see the pictures from on Facebook? Both begin in New York City and end in Long Beach, CA, but the two trips are completely different. In the map software trip, the journey is plotted on pure statistics. Do this then do this then do this. In Magnus's Excellent Adventure, Margaret and I planned a fun mini-cation for Magnus that included state parks, a visit to Gateway Arch and the Grand Canyon, a side trip on historic Route 66, and a family visit. The difference is in the attention to detail. By focusing on her interests (hiking, history, and family), her husband's love of photography, and incorporating Magus's need for continuous exercise, we achieved her goal and arrived in California with a rested, fit dog and happy humans. Each side trip was well planned to benefit both people and Magnus.

Always remember that your dream is built on baby steps and these little tasks require a commitment of time, energy and resources but they also need a dash of passion to keep you motivated.

I'm extremely patient provided I get my own way in the end.
~Margaret Thatcher

Final Thoughts

Goal planning is an incredibly useful tool. It creates control over a complex process and builds confidence in the person who finishes his or her well laid out plan. There are, however, a few pitfalls.

The cliff. A goal plan works because it structures and directs your efforts toward a dream. When you complete a major goal or dream, it is often very disorienting. Suddenly, after four or five months or more of motivated effort, you are goal-less. This is an uncomfortable feeling but very natural and normal. Give yourself time to adjust and take some recovery time. If necessary, think of the week or month after your completed goal or dream as required rest time. Once you've had a chance to regroup both mentally and physically, you will quickly reorient on a new goal or dream. If you get stuck and feel like you're floundering, go buy another lottery ticket and see what dream surfaces!

Injuries and bumps in the road. Life happens and as a professional, semi-professional or amateur athlete so will injuries. Disruptions and injuries are part of the journey. There is no way to incorporate them into a goal plan since they're completely unpredictable! Unfortunately, they seem so much worse when you have a plan laid out and then cannot implement it.

When you encounter an interruption or problem that prevents you from working your goal plan – be it an injury to yourself or your dog or a work complication or a family issue – just make the adjustment. It's okay to be angry and disappointed that your previous hard work and all your planning is now on hold or cancelled. However, it is rare that you must give up your dream.

> *Goals give you direction.*
> *Direction gives you results.*
> *Results give you confidence.*

When you layout your goals and tasks and then begin to work the plan, you have a micro focus. You are targeted in on the nitty-gritty. With an injury or life disruption, you must consciously change back to a macro focus. Look at the big picture. You will heal. Your dog will heal. Another job will come along or you'll find a new career. Family life will eventually settle down into a new normal.

Summon up the dream and expand your timeframes away from the day or week to a year or two. Perhaps some dust will build up on your goal plan but the dream is still real and often attainable.

Small deeds done are better than
great deeds planned.
~ Peter Marshall

Half-Assed

Half-assed [haf-ast] adjective: refers to having a desired goal while consciously choosing not to put in the necessary effort to actually achieve it.

It's one thing to say you have dreams. It's another to say you are trying to achieve your dreams. Yet, it is an entirely different thing to actually achieve them. The fragile line between these three stages is broken with effort. It isn't enough to half-ass your way to your goals. If anything you need to get your rear end in high gear. No ifs, ands, or butts about it. If you want to achieve your goals, you won't just try. You won't crack under pressure. You won't assume you can do it. You'll put effort behind everything you do until you excel.

The difference between try and triumph is a little umph.

Agility and Beyond Blog - Kathleen Oswald - May 13, 2013

Never retreat. Never explain.
Get it done and let them howl.
~ Benjamin Lowerr

2014 AKC International Team Tryouts
Kathleen & Whimzy

#4
Confidence

The fourth "C" of the *muscles-over-mind* system is confidence. Confidence cannot be bought, given, traded or absorbed. It must be earned and then owned. Confidence is frequently discussed in conjunction with sports competitions but it is not exactly easy to define. So, what is confidence?

For competitive athletes, confidence is....

A solid belief in your ability to get things done. Confidence requires effort. Sometimes progress is simply a continuous series of little failures followed by success. Sometimes we have a big one-time improvement. Either way, it is the effort behind the improvement that builds a belief in your ability that you can do anything.

The classic example of this is a puppy learning to run. Puppies roll, slide, stand, stumble, and kind of go splat a lot but they always get up and try again. They have a goal – to run – and they just keep plugging away at it until they succeed. With each attempt, they improve. Some days more than others but they steadily improve.

Confidence requires this progression.

You must set a specific goal and then make steady, continuous efforts to achieve it. Think about climbing a mountain. You start at the bottom and just keep stepping upward until you reach the top. It doesn't matter how many times you stop and rest so long as you resume going up. Any time you work toward a stated goal, you are climbing. You are building confidence. When you set your sights on a goal, it is the small slips and mistakes, regroups, and then motion forward that builds the knowledge that you can do it!

When you strive for success – whether you get there or not – you are creating an ingrained belief that you can do it. Confidence comes from *knowing* you can do it.

> Confidence is built on the relationship between success and failure. Failure can only occur when success is attainable. Success is defined by the degree of failure possible.

Acknowledge your improvements. For confidence, it is the acknowledgement and recognition of accomplishments that counts. When you set a goal, you must pay attention to your effort and the progress which results. Without awareness, there is no change in your confidence level. This concept ties closely to the need to maintain a daily log. It is absolutely your best record of effort and every entry generates a little more confidence.

Lucky versus successful. Think of the difference between money earned through a random lottery win and the sale of a company that you built. Both provide financial stability but you cannot earn confidence from a lottery win. You might feel joy, relief and be stress-free but there's no confidence in a lottery win. Creating and nurturing a business with the inevitable successes and failures as it grew and became established can provide you with unlimited confidence. Even if the construction of your company was smooth and relatively easy, you still achieved something substantial which developed from a belief in yourself. Interestingly, the same is also true if the business fails. You still gain confidence. It might take awhile to find it and feel it but it is there for you.

Alternately, if you succeed but attribute your success to luck, then you've missed an opportunity to strengthen your confidence. You must accept that it is your efforts that created the accomplishment (big or small). Effort does not have to be difficult or painful. It just needs to be progress with intention.

A feeling, a state of mind. Confidence is a concept, but more than that, confidence is an emotion. When you know that you can be competitive, that you are prepared, and that you can win, it shows in your attitude and your body language. What we see in the relaxed, calm demeanor of the experienced, seasoned competitor is an expression of confidence. It is not arrogance or egoism. Confidence is quiet and calm but it is also a visible state of mind.

Ego and hype are loud and very visible. When an athlete or performer is being egoistic, it is does not look like confidence. The experienced, thoughtful athlete knows that success comes from within and is humbled by the journey he or she is taking with their dog. True confidence is wrapped in thankfulness and humility and this separates it from egotistical behaviors by a long country mile!

Side benefits. The first side-benefit from confidence is emotional resilience. With a belief in the process - success generated from conscious effort - your ability to handle a few disruptions and disappointments improves substantially. Setbacks and difficulties just become part of the process and you can rebalance emotionally and move forward much quicker. Confidence does not take away disappointment. It just gives you a tool to break through it faster.

Another side benefit is a bit of mental flexibility. When you live confidently, you will discover alternate solutions quicker. After a defeat or mistake, the way forward becomes clearer sooner. The loss or breakdown is still there but you'll be quicker to step over it and move upward and on.

Cannot ignore or defeat fear. For competitors, fear is always present, particularly at major events or as you are about to complete a quest. Fear manifests as tension in the muscles and static in the brain. Your mind gets consumed with worries, doubt and disaster scenarios and your ability to function is blown away. Because fear invades both your muscles and your mind, it is particularly difficult to eliminate. Confidence is the antidote to this shutdown process. It gives you the perspective and knowledge to reset from a state of fear or doubt to relaxed and calm.

We gain strength, and courage, and confidence by each experience in which we really stop to look fear in the face...we must do that which we think we cannot.
~Eleanor Roosevelt

Always elusive. When untended, it will flow in and out of your psyche at random. One weekend it will be strong and reliable; the next not so much. As with much of the *muscles-over-mind* system, our goal is to teach you specific exercises for gaining control over the mind's whims. You can build, manage and control your confidence levels.

In order to create and then maintain a steady level of confidence in all your competitive endeavors, we have several different paths to explore. Each of the following sections explores an aspect of confidence – how it is created, how it is worn down and how it is maintained for life.

- Thought Awareness

- Terminate the ANTs

- Defeat Fear and Anxiety

- Create a Positive Mental Environment

Silence is a source of great strength.
~ Lao Tzu

Thought Awareness

The acclaimed psychologist and creator of the hierarchy of needs theory, Abraham Maslow, stated "What is necessary to change a person is to change his awareness of himself." Awareness is simply knowledge. Gaining knowledge (aka learning) about breed lines, sheep shearing, disc flight patterns, grooming techniques, animal behavior, or new rally signs is really quite easy. Learning about ourselves - becoming more self-aware - is a bit different and often more difficult. Self-awareness requires quiet introspection and it can be uncomfortable at times. However, confidence begins and ends inside your head, so you must become very aware of the thoughts bouncing around in there!

In order to be tuned into your thoughts, you must first be grounded in the present and second you must be consciously observant of your own thinking.

With your work thru the first three C's of the *muscles-over-mind* system, you now have several skills to shift your focus into the present moment and keep it there. Being in the present moment, allows you to focus on your thoughts and words. It is also a mental state that allows you to be aware without being critical or analytical. Internal, mental awareness requires you to observe but not judge.

The ability to simply observe – to see without thought – is a skill lost to many adults. Children see without judging or categorizing all the time. As adults we analyze, compare and judge. Basically, we think too much! Awareness of thought is different from changing or correcting thoughts. It is too easy to become your own worst critic. This is not the pathway to confidence. We need to relearn or refresh the ability to observe – to just be aware.

As competitive dog trainers, we have multiple tools to enhance our physical awareness. Obedience and rally training facilities often have large mirrors along one side of the room. These provide handlers with a real-time image of their body position. Executing halts, turns or pivots in front of the mirror gives the handler immediate feedback. Much like a young ballet dancer performing on the bar, every move is choreographed and studied from fingertip to toenail. With the mirror, you can enhance awareness by exaggerating a motion, slowing a move down, or having an instructor physically guide your body through the movement. Another popular tool to enhance body awareness is video tape. The advantage of video is endless. You can watch it in slow motion. You can watch it after your performance for immediate feedback and you can analyze it later for specific, smaller training issues. You can also use video to track your improvements or catch small changes before they settle into permanence. A good instructor or coach can also provide invaluable insight into your motions and actions, both in class and in the ring. Functioning as impartial eyes, an instructor can tell you what he or she sees as you perform.

As competitors, many of you have used these tools and probably several others to increase physical awareness. As you progressed through the training levels, your awareness of body position changed by degrees - from the whole arm down to a specific finger position. This level of physical awareness is necessary to master a sport and is often what we demand of our canine partners without being aware of our own. A lot of us use the physical awareness tools daily but what about mental awareness? What tools have you been taught to improve awareness of your thoughts much less fine tune them for excellence?

As you might expect, enhancing thought awareness is a bit tricky. You typically have around 50,000 thoughts a day. This is roughly 7,000 for each waking hour. Obviously, you cannot become *aware* of 50,000 thoughts a day. Talk about a headache!

Fortunately, most thoughts are effortless, maintenance-like, and can wash through your consciousness harmlessly. Daily functions - from feeding the dogs to baking treats to chatting on the phone to answering emails — are done by habit. As we discussed, actions repeated multiple times become habitual behaviors, which are under unconscious thought control and require minimal mental effort. Your brain is wired to do this and it is an important feature that lets you function in today's society.

> All thoughts are not created equal.

Furthermore, every day, normal living thoughts happen but do not require awareness unless you specifically want to change the associated behavior. These are the mostly unconscious thoughts we use to get dressed, drive to work, buy groceries, pay bills, and get your house cleaned. The same is true about your organizational thoughts, which get you to work on time, remember to bake dog treats for the trial on Saturday, or do the laundry so you have clean clothes on Monday morning. These are simply existence thoughts and should just flow along without interference.

The remaining thoughts - more than a few thousand a day - are a large part of who you are and how you deal with your world. These are the thoughts over which you need awareness.

Where to begin thought awareness is a good question. Obviously, we cannot use a mirror or video camera. You can pay for a therapist to explore your thoughts with you but that may take a few years! For most competitive athletes who want to simply gain enough awareness of their thinking to build their own self-esteem and confidence, enhancing thought awareness can be a fairly simple process. You just need to tune-in, review and then evaluate the thoughts in your mind.

Kathleen and I ask our students to do the following three steps to improve their thought awareness.

Step 1 - Tune in. Really *listen* to the chatter in your head. Think of your thought streams as a radio station that is online in your head 24/7. Spend a couple days being aware of your thoughts. Observe only. You may be amazed at what goes on in your own mind! Again, we come back to the concept of your mind as multiple entities. Try to notice thoughts as they occur, particularly during quiet times like when walking your dog or driving to a training class and pay extra attention to your daydreams.

After a few days, speak your thoughts out loud or at least think about verbalizing them. Talking out loud in public may get you a visit with a doctor who has a comfy couch or a funny looking jacket for you to try on! If you were to announce your thoughts to the world, would they make sense? Would you talk to a friend or your dog in the same tone you are using in your mind? Would you present the same message? When you daydream are you having fun and success or are you running disaster scenarios?

Step 2 – Review. Once you are successful at tuning into and listening to the chatter in your head, spend a few days or a week truly reviewing and inspecting your thought content. If it helps to keep an active record, then create a simple chart. Each day categorize your thoughts about yourself and your activities as positive or negative. How are you talking to yourself, about yourself, and about your environment? Are your thoughts predominately positive or negative?

Step 3 – Identify thought patterns. Once you have proof of what's going on in your head. You can begin to analyze and identify thought patterns and habits. Consider whether your mental chatter is positive or negative. If your thoughts are positive and uplifting, then repeat them to yourself. Write them down. If your thoughts are negative, then a change is needed. With a tune-in skill, you can begin to use a mental filter. Most thoughts should pass effortlessly through the filter. Negative thoughts should be trapped for review and/or elimination. You should also listen carefully to the people around you. Are they negative-trash talkers or positive and motivational?

Workout Phraseology

When I began working with my personal trainer, Walter Santos, it didn't take long before I discovered that we had very different definitions for the word "fun" and that he tended to use what I consider to be upside-down talk. These are comments that are meant as encouragement but are really negative for the recipient. For example, in the beginning he had several favorite phrases that I truly despised, "Keep going this is the hard part," or "The next set is even tougher, " or "You're going to like today's workout. It's really difficult." Sheesh. It's truly a wonder on more than one day that he didn't get bopped with the kettle bell I was swinging!

Of course, coaches frequently inspire athletes with a slightly negative comment. It can be motivational. I found immediately that much prefer positive chatter. It took a few months but Walter did change his rhetoric. I now hear "You can do it," or "This set is a good challenge for you," or "Nice!" Unfortunately, I now have a deeply ingrained negative emotional trigger to "Nice!" since Walter only says it when my muscles are shaking and sweat is dripping off me like a tropical rainstorm!

Terminate the ANTs

As your thought awareness filter takes shape, you will improve quickly at identifying positive versus negative thoughts. Positive thoughts translate into physical energy and improved confidence. We like those! On the other hand, negative thinking drains energy and reduces confidence. Our goal is to reduce the negative thoughts in your head as much as possible. Like weeds in a garden, they tend to come back but with a thought awareness filter working, you can find and eliminate them quickly!

Remember, your brain is wired to use habits – both physical and mental. When you think or do something consistently like keyboarding or writing checks for training classes, your brain wires that action or thought into permanent existence. It actually changes the physiology around the neuron to make it more efficient and faster. So, if you habitually think negative, your brain becomes wired for negative. Of course, the opposite is also very true. If you think positive, your brain becomes wired for positive!

Negative thoughts = brain pollution.
~Jane Savoie

One of the best explanations of negative thinking as a habit that we have heard or read is in Dr. Amen's book *Change Your Brain, Change Your Life*. In the book and in his lecture series, Dr. Amen discusses habitual thinking and notes that much of it is negative. He created the concept of Automatic Negative Thoughts or ANTs to describe this thinking pattern. Dr. Amen categorizes habitual negative thinking into nine ANTs. While all nine of the ANTs that Dr. Amen identifies are worth exploring, there are three that deserve particular consideration for competitive athletes.

ANT - Always or Never. Catch every occurrence of *always* or *never* that flows through your thoughts. Both *always* and *never* are huge generalizations and frequently preface a negative statement. Whenever you say or think *always* or *never*, alarm bells should go off.

Not too long ago, one of my students greeted me early in the morning at a local agility trial. When I asked, "How does the course look?" Suzie replied, "Doesn't matter. I never qualify in that ring." Wow! I pulled in a few deep breaths and asked her to explore the never ANT. We discussed what was behind the negativity. Was "never" a correct adjective or an exaggeration? Was there a specific training issue that we had not prepared for? The building we were in contained two indoor soccer fields with lines and circles on the turf, as well as large posters on the walls. Some dogs, particularly young ones, react to these distractions. Suzie took one look and sunk into a negative funk.

With some creative thinking, we modified her course plan and incorporated some unusual handling moves to avoid the trouble spots (literally) and she pulled out a qualifying run in Masters Jumpers. Rather than let the never set her up for failure, we were able to work out a plan for success.

Any time you use a qualifier, like *always* (or its relatives: regularly, perpetually, or constantly), you need to catch it in your thought awareness filter and examine it. Take a moment to dissect the thought. Evaluate the statement for validity and truth. These types of thoughts are often negative exaggerations and this is particularly true when you use *never* - or it's relatives like not ever, don't hold your breath or not happening - in conjunction with expectations or goals. On the other hand, if it is a true statement or thought, then there is an issue, whether it is training, preparation, or scheduling, that should be addressed.

Defying the Odds

Defy the odds. Overcome all the obstacles. Don't let anything or anyone hold you back. Triumph over challenges and reach up and snatch your goals right out of the air. To defy the odds is the classic story of the underdog. These are the stories that inspire us.

Viewing challenges as obstacles is just wrong. We're on a journey not in a battle. Competitions aren't "tests" to be won, but lessons to be learned from. You cannot conquer your way to your dreams. Rather than simply reaching your dream, become what you've always dreamt of. The odds that seem to be against you are simply opportunities waiting to be turned into advantages. Challenges aren't meant to hold you back but propel you forward. If it doesn't challenge you, then it isn't going to change you. You cannot start and end your journey as the same person. Change allows us to become the person we've always wanted to be. It allows us to be the best we can be.

Agility & Beyond Blog - Kathleen Oswald - April 28, 2013

ANT - Focus on the negative. Having a bad day? When faced with a challenging or difficult situation, it is way too easy to put a negative spin on the entire day's efforts, project or event. Do not let problems, difficulties or negative encounters occupying your thoughts for a long time or – God forbid – a whole day! Deal with them and move on. Everyone has to deal with traffic jams, lost equipment, inclement weather and unfriendly competitors. Handle the problem and then go do something else.

There are times when you may have to make a conscious effort to continue living in the present. Recognize that it was a difficult situation or unpleasant moment and then let the unfortunate event slide into the past. You do not need to let those moments color your whole day or demeanor. Try adopting your dog's method! Dogs literally shake away bad events and get right back to the fun!

Since we compete with a partner, sometimes it is okay to call "Uncle!" If the negative event or situation is so disturbing, please let yourself call it quits for the day. We have several students who work the night shift at the hospital. Some mornings, the intensity and demand of the job these doctors or nurses do is written on their faces. On those days, we change what exercises they do with their dog or Kathleen or I trains their pup that day. They need time to adjust and de-perk. Coming to class with their dog for exercise and entertainment is vastly different from them trying to train. Your dog can never understand your emotional upset, so you owe it to him or her to know when not to train or compete. Taking a day off or just going for a long walk through the park is just fine. Your dog will benefit from your acknowledgement that the negative thoughts will take time to dissipate.

ANT - Fortune telling. Disaster daydreaming is a favorite pastime of negative thinkers. With just a touch of encouragement, our brains seem thrilled to dream up calamities for the foreseeable future. If you consistently daydream in the negative, you need to stop. Capture and halt the negative scenario and remake the daydream into a positive, enjoyable story. Initially, the conversion of negative fortune telling or daydreaming may take some effort but it is important to stop as much negative thinking as possible. Let yourself triumph over your imagined adversity. Why not have big wonderful dreams?

> *You can wire your brain for positive thinking.*

Shake It Off!

Watch your dogs carefully next time they tussle over a favorite toy. Demon and my Lhasa, Jack, often decide they both want the same squeaky toy during play time and obviously only one can win. There's usually a bit of grumbling and shoving but Jack almost always wins. He's a stubborn little dude! This leaves Demon without a toy. What does he do? He shakes – literally! It's a very common dog behavior. Dogs literally shake from head-to-tail and this instantly resets their mental attitude. After a good shake, Demon generally bounces back to me and – being a sheltie – he barks at me to go find him another toy! He doesn't bother Jack. He doesn't fuss about the lost toy. He gets back to having fun and engaging with me.

Discovering any of these three ANTs working in your mind is a simple way to help you build a screen for thought awareness. It makes your filter easier to create. As Dr. Amen points out, all of these ANTs are just bad mental habits but any habit can be changed once the behavior is identified. Awareness is the beginning of change.

Listening in on your private thoughts and dialogues is a very strong, positive habit. Eliminating negative thoughts requires diligence and attention but the effort is worth it. You cannot be confident with a negative thought stream flowing through your head. You need a positive, affirming thought stream. For some, this is a natural state. For others, positive thinking needs to become a new, good habit.

> The only difference between fear and excitement is whether you are breathing.
> ~Dan Millman

Defeat Fear and Anxiety

Confidence does not actually defeat fear. Confidence lets you function *through* fear and anxiety. Even the most experienced competitors with a big tournament on the line will feel anxious and afraid. It's part of what makes competitions exciting and entertaining. Without that emotional connection, few of us would compete. Of course, the fear must be managed and that is a whole lot easier to say than do!

In order to begin the process of managing fear, we always ask our students to spend a minute to think about fear. What is it? Fear is a survival instinct. And, it is important to note that it is literally hardwired into your brain. The instantaneous, physical response to fear by-passes conscious thought. For millennium, the human body's reaction to fear needed to be faster – much, much faster - than thought. Even in the not too distant past, the caveman who reacted to the sudden appearance of a saber tooth cat with an instantaneous (fear-based) response lived much longer than the caveman who took a moment to think about the danger the big cat presented. The thoughtful caveman made a nice lunch for the saber tooth cat and had less opportunity to produce and raise kids.

In our present world, we rarely need these instinctive reactions but they're definitely part of our evolution and still functional. A fear response is part of being alive. It is as natural as smiling. How you think about a fear response is a different issue.

Check your Breathing

Fear has its own breathing pattern. It is very different from excitement. Fear breathing is not just shallow or short. It is erratic and often involves holding your breath. Recognize fear-based breathing and interrupt it with a couple sets of 4-7-8 breathing.

When you accept that fear is normal, then you can begin to see that being anxious or afraid of an event or situation is not a tragedy. Fear has many distinct sources and can indicate many different things. Like any other emotion, there are multiple tools for handling fear and its partners in crime: doubt and anxiety.

Since fear is one of the biggest issues for competitors in any sport, we have collected and refined lots of different tools and ideas for managing it. Take time to explore each concept and incorporate the one(s) that work best for you, your situation or your current level of fear and anxiety. You may find one works well now and another will work for you in a future endeavor. Just remember to reach for control when a fear response starts and you'll do just fine!

Live big! Simply accept that many situations, decisions and competitions are going to generate fear. Any large endeavor should have some component of fear. Much of a competitive lifestyle or hobby – buying a puppy, changing instructors, attending a high-profile seminar, beginning a new sport, or qualifying for a tournament, traveling to a national or an international event – is somewhat risky and scary. Everyone feels anxious for some of these (if not all!).

As an athlete who is competing, being nervous means that you care about the outcome. Being worried or afraid means you are fully engaged and this is often when you are living big! Are you nervous about your first time in the ring or about your first major tournament? It's perfectly normal and means you are progressing forward in your sport and achieving success!

So, accept that you will be afraid, nervous or anxious and then get ahead of the emotion. When you accept that being nervous is a very good thing, it will lose much of its power.

If you can't accept losing, you can't win.
~Vince Lombardi

Accept all outcomes. Fear is an instinctive reaction to danger. Your body is hardwired to use fear to survive. Your mind, however, should not be cranking up a fear-reaction every time you think about competing or contemplate pushing your personal envelope with a new training methodology. A continuous dose of fear-reaction is counterproductive, disruptive and downright unhealthy.

In order to keep fear reactions in perspective, we teach our students to address the situations in their mind well before they put a stamp on the national's entry envelope or put that fancy new leash on their dog and enter the ring. The goal is to accept all outcomes – from total disaster to total success.

There are four simple steps to the process. It is important to work through all four to ensure that you do not get hung up on all the negatives. Think of this process as proofing. Obtaining a competition ready behavior from your dog involves: introduction, training and then proofing. This is the same process that we utilize for reducing anxiety. By considering or entering an event that causes stress, you've introduced fear. So, the next step is to train your mind (while on a walk or on the couch) to accept the fear as normal. The last step, which is described here, is to make it harder than it probably will be (proofing) so you're mind can learn how to adjust.

The steps to "proofing" for fear are:

Run a disaster scenario. Find some time to sit quietly or take your dog for a long walk and think thru all the possible outcomes for the event. Start with a phenomenal performance and then imagine mediocre and then run your absolute worst case failure. Let that fortune telling genie go ahead and create the most botched up, awful outcome you can. Then ask yourself a few basic questions. What will happen if you choke and fail? How will you feel about all the effort, time and resources if you don't win, place or even qualify? What will you say to your family, friends and co-workers? How can you face your training partners or classmates? Go through each conversation in your mind. Find the right words, attitude and tone to talk about the event as if it was a total disaster. Facing the disappointment and awkward conversations as part of your preparations will take away a huge amount of stress and worry. Since you already survived it in your mind, the reality – should it happened – can also be survived and then used as a learning experience.

> *Failure is always an option. Accepting this fact makes it much more likely that you will be successful.*

Challenge the ridiculous. When we daydream, our imagination can get a bit carried away. When you imagined winning Nationals, did you immediately picture a spot on the Tonight Show? Or perhaps you daydreamed about being presented with a four-foot high trophy at your next club banquet? Your imagination might have gone too far! Sure you'll have fun celebrating with your friends and family but it probably won't involve an appearance on the late night TV or having an indoor arena named after your dog. Alternately, when you suffered through a resounding defeat, did you envision having to relocate with the witness protection program or having to switch to training cats? Again your imagination needs some brakes.

Accept all the scenarios as possible. This is extremely important since fear is often a case of being overly worried about the unknown. If a win is possible, then so is a failure. Accept failure as a necessary part of the process. Having a high tolerance for failure is a key characteristic for high-achievers. When you are comfortable with both outcomes, they become equalized. Fear cannot immobilize you when you already have a plan in place to handle it.

All of us put considerable time, energy and resources into our dog competitions but in reality our success/failure is not life altering. Will missing the cut for Finals at Nationals change your friendships? Alter your projects list or prospects for a promotion at work? Plunge you into bankruptcy? Require medical treatment or a hospital stay? Hopefully, you answered no to all of these. If you let the negative event or situation go and do not internalize it (make it who you are), then the experience fades quickly into the past where you can learn from it and move on.

Set your goals and expectations to the positive. Having imagined the best and worst possible outcomes for your event or situation, the last step of this process is to select the best and move on. We encourage our students to accept and handle the very real possibility of failure and then plan for total success. You can let go of the negative knowing that you have the tools/skills in place to deal with it and get moving on a solid plan for success. Select the positive and live with it as your new reality.

With confidence, you have won even
before you have started.
~ Marcus Garvey

Maintain a big picture view. Fear has a tendency to flood our minds. It takes over. Once loose in your thoughts, anxiety can make small life events seem large and all encompassing. Being anxious and afraid narrows your focus. Again, this is a simple survival mechanism and it was built into your brain by evolution. When your ancestral caveman was fighting that saber tooth cat, the caveman was not well served by a wandering mind. Total focus on escape was a big priority. The poor caveman whose brain took a moment to think about the survival of his species versus the cats' quite simply became that cat's lunch. A big picture view was not a good use of brain power! Needless to say, your genetic make-up does not include a process for big picture thinking while you are afraid or worried.

When you are anxious or distressed, you need to consciously shift from a micro focus to the macro picture. Dragging your thoughts away from its current obsession reduces fear. When you find your mind looping over-and-over through the same fear-inducing idea or plan, take a moment to get out of the bleak, depressing future your mind is stuck in. Use your 4-7-8 breathing to reconnect with the present or take a moment to revisit past successes to jump start a positive attitude.

Puzzling

As dog trainers, sometimes I feel as though we spend so much time looking forward that we overlook what we are working on today. The "big picture" gets blurry and we lose our understanding how each day of the journey will come together at the end. You can't put a puzzle together by simply staring at the picture on the box. You have to examine each piece and discover the unique connection it shares with the others. More than once you have to test a piece in different places before you get the right spot. At the beginning, each dog is a puzzle too. It takes time, patience, and a solid view of the "big picture" to try and figure out how all the little pieces can come together to be your both your best friend and your competition partner.

Agility & Beyond Blog – Kathleen Oswald – August 6, 2013

Put fears on a number scale. When you are truly stuck in a fear mode or anxiety is causing you to hyperventilate, try quantifying your anxiety. Pluck out each worry or fear and assign it a number from one to ten on a *lifetime* scale. Let one be a good impact and ten be a horrible outcome. What will having a horrible score at this trial mean to your life? Is this a ten or perhaps just a one or two? How will missing the cut for Nationals impact your life in four, six or ten years? Frequently, we let life's little bumps and disappointments grow in importance. A number scale can get them back into perspective. Time has a way of correcting and smoothing out the impact of problems but there's no need to wait. Do it now.

Own your success and throw away failures. Unfortunately, some of our students own their mistakes and attribute their successes to accidents or flukes. When Kathleen or I congratulate them on a good run or practice set, they make an excuse for their success. They brush aside our praise. It's important to reverse this thinking. Let your accomplishments be yours. This doesn't have to be an ego trip. You are allowed to bask in your achievements and pat yourself on the back for a job well done whether you've mastered a new skill or reached your dream.

Alternately, failures can be mistakes, accidents of fate, or simply misfortune. Analyze the mistake and learn why you made it so it won't be repeated. Recognize the bad luck of a slip that caused a bar to come down and shrug it off. Accept that a curious sparrow on the ring fencing caused your dog to momentarily lose attention during the signal exercise and chuckle at life's whims. Whatever the reason for the failure, accept the lesson and then throw it away. Your dog already did!

Many people limit themselves to what they think they can do. You can go as far as your mind lets you. What you believe, remember, you can achieve.
~ Mary Kay Ash

The Art of Losing

The art of losing comes from understanding that no one is the best. There is always something that can be improved upon; even world champions place second sometimes. I have yet to meet a team with a one hundred percent qualification rate, much less someone who wins one hundred percent of the time. We can only ever be the best we can be, and personally I believe that "losing" only makes us better. Agility competitions are a clock and a course. Other handlers aren't competition. They are mentors, teachers, examples, research and friends. Although they may not realize it, they are all those things and much more. Without them, I'd never push my handling. Without them, I wouldn't race against the clock. Without them, I'd never strive to be better or know what I was capable of. You can lose to a clock and a course. You can only learn from those you run against.

"Losing" is only a negative term if you're focused on ribbon-based results. The reality is that you cannot lose with the correct mindset. Placing low, or even getting disqualified, is not losing. It is an educational experience. You learn where you can be more efficient, faster, which skills you need to train or, at the very least, you are humbled for a moment.

No matter how good you are, you are not perfect. But who would want to be? Imperfections are what motivate us. If you couldn't get better, you'd never try. It's our flaws that propel us forward.

Agility & Beyond Blog – Kathleen Oswald – January 20, 2014

Use a goal plan. Not only will a goal plan keep you motivated and focused, it provides a huge antidote to fear and doubt. Working your goal plan builds confidence. When you climb a massive set of stairs or a couple hundred pyramid steps, you can look down and see how far you've risen. It's uplifting to see the progress and to know you climbed every inch. The same sense of accomplishment comes from completing a detailed goal plan. The process of setting goals and working specific tasks to attain your dream is a major component to creating confidence. With a detailed plan, you have a paper "staircase" that shows your efforts and progress. It also lets you accept that success as your own.

With a trail of acknowledged successes behind you, each new challenge that raises your fear or anxiety level will be just a little bit easier to face. You'll have the perspective to know that you beat the odds once before. Why not again? And again? And again?

Fear is also reduced when you use your goal plan to scale back the size and scope of your project. Obtaining enough OTCH points to qualify for nationals might seem huge and scary when you dream about it. However, if you lay out the journey and eventually break that down to earning ten or fifteen points per trial, then that's doable.

Become your hero. Another way to destroy anxiety is to adopt the attitude of someone more accomplished. Pay attention to your hero (someone you admire), a mentor, or your coach. You cannot become someone else but you can adopt their behaviors! The physical motions and body positions that manifest from a confident attitude can be mimicked.

Notice your hero's energy level and words. What does she say and how does it sound? Does your hero, mentor or coach sound excited and nervous or calm and humorous? Study her habits and body language. Stand up straight. Smile. Smooth out your walk into a confident stroll. Lower your voice and talk slowly. All of these are typical body-language behaviors of the inherently confident competitor. Adopt them and your anxiety will go down. Doubt will dissipate with every smile and panic will plummet when you can laugh. Remember your body can talk to your mind. If you walk the walk of someone more confident, you'll be influencing your thoughts. They'll follow along with the concept of improved confidence.

Take your own journey. We all compete for different reasons and at different levels. Some of our students want to compete occasionally when the trial is close to home. Others want to compete in Europe against the best the agility world can produce for one weekend in the fall. Both – and every level in between – are perfectly fine. A goal is an individual endeavor. Occasionally, one of our students feels pressured to compete at a higher level than her time, resources and personal interest dictates. We actively work to prevent this!

Each of our students has a partnership with their dog. How it evolves and where or when that team trains or competes is unique. Not every team can or should compete for a National championship. Keep your dreams front and center so you don't add stress and breakdown your confidence by reaching for someone else's.

Wherever you go, go with all your heart.
~Confucius

Set realistic expectations. Disappointment is the point where results meet expectations and the results fall short. Anxiety is often simply the fear of disappointment.

When you keep track of your efforts, note your progress, and move steadily toward your dream, you will have the ability to set realistic expectations. With a true picture (not a wish or an extravagant daydream) of your current skills and competitive levels, you can avoid a lot of fear and anxiety. Why stress over a run in the Finals when your existing skill set is not going to get you there? Not sure of your level? Seek out a fellow competitor or instructor who has the ability to evaluate your skills and be brutally honest with you. They may tell you that you're not ready or they may tell you that you've been holding back! Either way you need to set yourself up for success by setting realistic expectations.

Realistic expectations do not interfere with your dream. They improve the process by keeping you focused on the present where you can train for improvement and keep your confidence high.

Ask a good question. All of these fear reduction techniques are valuable and can be applied to almost any situation, whether it's a nosework trial, tracking test, or a cancer screening. However, we are human and sometimes a fear reaction just gets rolling. In his book, *Ten Minute Toughness*, Jason Selk describes a way to deal with setbacks or obstacles that suddenly seem insurmountable. When you find yourself crushed and mentally aground, ask a simple question, "What is the one thing that I can do right now to make this better?"

This question-and-answer habit is useful for fear-induced panic and extreme disappointment. It brings your focus back to the present moment and gives your mind something concrete to lock onto. The answer may be as simple as make a list of things to pack to go home, take a long walk, hug your dog, get lunch, or review your videotape. Asking the question is the important part. It is the first step back to a calm, relaxed state.

The ones who want to achieve and win championships motivate themselves.
~ Mike Ditka

Create a Positive Mental Environment

The foundation under confidence is a positive attitude.

Being positive is more a lifestyle choice than an attitude. No one is positive all day, every day. Everyone has bad days and negative moments. If you are the exception to this rule, then you are very blessed! We all have vet bills, missing leashes, bad training days, even worse trial days, and poop to clean up. Life happens and we all lose our temper, get disappointed or find our sport frustrating at times. It doesn't really matter how you handle these little events. Go ahead and be annoyed or angry. Positive doesn't mean 24/7. It just means when you calm down or get a choice, you find the positive idea, thought or plan.

Unfortunately, negative messages, attitudes and people surround us. It is up to you to build and then maintain a positive mental environment. We use several techniques to manage our space (home, office and training areas) and keep as many thoughts as possible pitched toward the positive.

Affirmations. Affirmations are positive statements or declarations. There are many different types of affirmations and they are useful for any personal development quest on which you embark. In fact, there are books and entire websites that specialize in affirmations for relationships, health, diet, spiritual quests, business success and many other topics.

Do a quick Internet search for "confidence affirmations." The last time we did the search, Kathleen and I got well over two million hits. There are a lot of people out there using affirmations for confidence! Many sport psychology books also have affirmations for competitive athletes. Your job, as you scan the Internet or read a motivational book, is to collect a long list of affirmations. With a wide variety and extensive list, you can select and change the statements so they work for you in your current situation. When building your list of positive statements, keep in mind the following:

It must valid for your sport. If the statement is not appropriate for you or dog competitions, then skip it. For example, in dog sports, we rarely have team-based competition with coaches so the affirmation "I have the best coaching," probably isn't a valid affirmation.

It must be true for you. You must also find affirmations that are true statements for you. Some statements may appeal to you but they may not be true. For example, the affirmation, "I am the star. It's my time shine bright," may sound good but in your heart it's not quite you. Being confident and having a high self-esteem level does not mean you have to be a star. However, if one day you want to be the one at the top of the podium, then include the affirmation on your list. If the statement is close, feel free to modify it, like "My dog is a star. I am his partner so he can shine." Affirmations are personal, positive statements for your use. Changing the statement doesn't break any rules.

It must apply to you. Sometimes we find an affirmation that prods us to change how we act or think but may not apply directly to our current situation. When this happens, there are two steps to be taken. First, modify the affirmation for your current position and second build in a plan to get to the first affirmation. For example, "I am in the best shape of my life," may not be true. However, if it resonates with you and you know that being in better shape will enhance your competitive experience, then you should (1) create an affirmation for your present situation and (2) go back to your personal (vs performance) goal plan and incorporate more fitness training. So, your affirmation becomes "My fitness is improving daily" and a new personal task can be a 20-minute workout four times per week.

> An affirmation opens the door. It's a beginning point on the path to change.
> ~Louise L. Hay

Affirmations work in multiple ways. First, they declare your right to be successful and confident. Second they confirm your ability to improve and enhance your training and your dog's. And, finally, they focus your mind on your dreams.

Some of our favorite affirmations are…

- I love and respect myself.
- I can achieve my dream.
- I improve every day.
- I am prepared, focused, and ready to compete in today's event.
- Today I will compete with strength, grace and consistency.
- It's all about my dog
- I am here to compete.
- Success is what I do.
- Today I feel great.
- I believe in myself.

Once you've found your positive self-statements, you have to put them to work. Affirmations succeed by giving your conscious mind a continuous dose of positive thinking. You now know that your subconscious mind will work hard to do what the conscious mind thinks. An affirmation like, "My fitness is improving daily," makes a great prompt to exercise every day. Affirmations are particularly effective when used first thing in the morning to set the tone of your day and right before you fall asleep. Many world class and professional athletes say them all day.

As you find or create affirmations, categorize them so they work within your goal plan. One of the best ways to use affirmations is to select a weak area in your training or mental management and then find affirmative statements to support the improved belief. For example, if you lack confidence on trial days, then search out self-esteem or confidence building affirmations. If you worry about your ability to commit to a long term project or goal, then seek out affirmations about persistence and perseverance. If you want to be healthier, find affirmations for health and vitality.

The best part about affirmations is how easy they are to use. We give our students the following guidelines for selecting, creating and using affirmations.

State in the first person. Affirmations are statements or declarations that are true and valid for you. In order to change your mental state or opinion of yourself or a situation, you must believe in the declaration. Make all your affirmations in the first person (I, me, my) so they apply to you and are about you. Some good examples…

- My mind is at peace.
- I am worthy of success.
- I am prepared and ready for this competition.
- I feel strong and healthy.
- I am a deserving of good fortune.

Make the message positive. Not all affirmations are positive. Many have embedded limits or are stated in the negative. Scan and avoid any affirmation that contains words that imply negativity or failure. For example, the statement, "I embrace my fears fully and calmly," sends a very mixed message and has a definite focus on fear. Well stated affirmations avoid words like no, don't, hate, bad or fear. For example, consider the affirmation, "I can overcome this obstacle." This statement is weak and with the use of "can" versus "will" almost implies a chance of failure. A much better affirmation is, "I will triumph over every adversity in my way." It is much stronger and pitches a positive message with active verbs.

Facebook

One of the best tools for maintaining a positive environment is to join the Facebook community. It's an amazingly positive world. Friends and family can be supportive, friendly and humorous. Kathleen and I have an overlapping friend network, within which there are literally dozens of positive posts every day. Short stories, affirmations, comments and "likes" appear all day to keep everyone's spirits high and to handle adversity. If your FB community isn't gushing with positive thoughts and ideas, then build a new one!

Use short sentences. The best affirmations are easy to remember and are quick to repeat or write. Try saying this affirmation three times, "I am too big a gift to the world to waste my time on self-pity and sadness." Compare it to saying, "I am unique and live joyously." Since, you should be thinking or saying your current affirmation(s) frequently, short sentences are best. It is also important that the declaration be concise and flow smoothly. Test out this affirmation, "I let go of my fears and worries that drain my energy for no good return." Not only is it swimming in negative, it is awkward. If you have to reread a statement to understand it, then move on to a better choice or reword it.

Select strong action verbs. Search for or create affirmations that have positive words and actions. A weak or bland verb will not resonate with your soul. Avoid words like happy, help, safe, good, attempt, try or content. When you build your affirmation list, collect statements that have strong, positive words like joy, love, achieve, strength, vitality, beautiful, unique, gift, etc. If you find an affirmative belief that is soft or vague, spice it up with your own words. For example, I took the declaration, "I believe in myself," and changed it to "I have unique talents and I believe in their power." Some examples of affirmations with strong verbs are:

- I am worthy of victory.
- I am deeply fulfilled.
- My dream is exciting and energizing.
- I feel powerful and prepared.
- My mind is sharp. My heart is open. My spirit is joyous.

Use multiple affirmations. You can definitely have more than one affirmation at a time. Many people use a short list of seven or eight. Be cautious about how many beliefs you try to alter at one time however. Change happens with time so focus on one or two beliefs that you want to change and select affirmations for just those weak areas. For best results, we like our student's affirmations to be closely aligned with their performance and personal goals. Since the goal plan is setup for a period of three to six months, they work one set of affirmations for ninety to one hundred eighty days, which is perfect. Always keep in mind that new habits take around one hundred days to become permanent!

Incorporate into daily life. Your affirmations should be repeated once a day (or more) to yourself. You can think, whisper, shout or chant them. You can also write them down. Think of your dream statement. It is an affirmation. You can also place your affirmations where you'll see and read them frequently. Many people find that the best way to get your subconscious to truly embrace the new affirmative belief is to state it three times in a row. Either say each affirmation on your list three times in a row or say your affirmation list three times.

Incorporate into your competitive routine. We also like our students to select one affirmation for confidence building. This affirmation will be incorporated into the mental management routine that they'll use at a competition, which we explain in the last section. The confidence affirmation must powerful. Some of our favorites are:

- I am prepared and ready for this competition.
- My accomplishments are my own.
- I am a dominant competitive force.
- Today is for me.
- I am a person of worth and value and I enjoy my success.

When you have confidence, you can have a lot of fun. And when you have fun, you can do amazing things.
~Joe Namath

Positive Messages. Another way to maintain a positive mental attitude is to surround yourself with positive messages. Put positive messages EVERYWHERE! Think of it as balancing out the negative that each of us inevitably encounters every day in our conversations and in the news.

Place positive statements on your desk, in the kitchen, in your car, on your walls, on the computer screen, and everywhere in between. It is also important to swap them every few weeks. You will only read them a few times before your eye will go right over them. In order to keep the messages fresh and mentally appealing, you need to move them frequently and also get new ones. Each statement should speak to you and give you a little burst of energy.

Some of our favorite phrases and inspirational quotes are scattered throughout this book. Some others are...

- The best way to get something done is to BEGIN.
- There is no elevator to success. You have to take the stairs.
- Positive minds live positive lives.
- Creativity is intelligence having fun.
- Optimism is a happiness magnet.
- A journey of a thousand miles begins with a single step.
- Live out your imagination, not your history.
- The best dreams happen when you're awake.
- Find the magic that makes your soul soar.
- Motivation is what gets you started. Habit is what keeps you going.
- Don't follow your dreams, chase them.
- What your mind can conceive, it can achieve.
- Life is like a roller coaster. It has its ups and downs but it's your choice to scream or enjoy the ride.
- Climb mountains not so the world can see you, but so you can see the world.

Can you imagine what I would do if I could do all I can?
~ Sun Tzu

Once you begin to look for positive statements and thoughts, you will find them everywhere: on the Internet, on your Facebook page, in books, on T-shirts, and in music lyrics, poems and movies. You can even find them in advertisements. Nike's phrase "Just Do It," is a timeless classic. When you find a good one, take time to write it down. Some will speak to you immediately; others may be more relevant at other times.

Keep interesting quotes, phrases or declarations stored in a file or folder – paper or electronic – so you can easily pick out new ones when you are starting a quest or just need a quick pick-me-up.

Your personal list of positive statements is also a good item to pack for major tournaments. Reading through a long list of positive concepts and ideas is a great antidote to case of nerves. It also makes great bed time reading. The last thing your mind hears before falling asleep is then a huge dose of positive thinking.

I he will to win, the desire to succeed, the urge to reach your full potential...these are the keys that will unlock the door to personal excellence.
~ Confucius

Positive Framing Technique. Life is not all roses, promotions, and birthday parties. Everyone has to deal with negative circumstances and disappointments. How you think and talk about life's normal bumps and your sports inherent problems can make a tremendous difference. Dog competitions should be fun and exciting.

We are not discussing or participating in brain surgery, legal maneuvers in front of the supreme court, or life-and-death situations in the ER, so a positive perspective and a bit of framing and creative labeling is perfect.

Rather than use the term, spin technique, which is a public relations concept used to manipulate public opinion, we encourage students to cultivate the habit of positive framing. . For example, we always encourage our competition clients to say "challenges" instead of "problems". Simply view and interpret life's events in a positive light. Framing means that you define every experience as positive, educational, or just part of your unique journey. Whenever something happens, select

> **The Kitchen Wall**
>
> When I discovered affirmations (love them!), I put them everywhere. My desk got a few picture statues so I could display affirmation cards and positive phrases easily. As a mom, I also spend a lot of time in the kitchen, so I painted one wall with whiteboard paint. All my favorite positive phrases and ideas are now on that wall and it is the focal point of the dining area. Kathleen faced that wall every night at dinner.

the positive. For example, if you skip a sign on a Rally course, you have two choices. The negative interpretation is "I screwed that up big." The positive framing point can be as simple as saying, "Well I need to memorize the course better!" Any mistake at a trial can be used as a learning experience. You just need to get past the emotion to the lesson.

Another common situation that needs positive framing skills is when you or your dog have an injury. Agility, obedience, rally, herding....these are competitive sports with two athletes. Injuries are a real part of any sport. When dealing with the inevitable training and trialing delay during the rest and recovery phases, keeping a positive mindset can be a major challenge. With a positive mental attitude, you can frame the situation many, many different ways. In 2009, when Demon was out of commission for eight weeks healing a jammed toe, I finally had the chance to really delve into mental management techniques. This book is a direct result of that injury. Neither I nor Kathleen would be the competitors we are today without those eight weeks of no or minimal agility training for Demon. I was disappointed to be icing his toe in the stands and not running the courses at the AKC Agility Nationals, but I also read four sport psychology books that weekend. With a positive mindset, I was able to frame his injury as a temporary setback that gave me time to investigate a new topic for my own personal development.

With positive framing as a life habit, failure has a completely different meaning. There have been many times during my competitive career that I actually set out to fail. Both Kathleen and I have told students to flunk more often! Failure means that you pushed yourself sufficiently hard to ensure future progress. Sometimes it is necessary to not succeed. Being able to embrace and accept failure is the mark of a balanced competitor.

Some specific suggestions for positive framing.....

- Actively listen to your self-talk and swap the negative to a positive. You can change problems into challenges. Failure becomes a lesson well learned. Screw-ups become opportunities to grow. Difficult people are characters. And, my favorite, nerves mean you are pushing out of your comfort zone.
- Monitor your conversations and direct them toward positive whenever possible. Be aware of those people around you who are consistently negative. Jane Savoie has a term for them. She refers to them as "stink'in thinkers." You may need to spend less time with these people!
- Replace every negative thought with a positive one.
- Be aware that all thoughts are not created equal; many thoughts only gain credibility through repetition.
- Accept only the positive. Even if you do slip into a negative mindset, acknowledge it and simply end with a positive comment or thought even if it's only a little one.

You just can't beat the person who
never gives up.
~Babe Ruth

Demon – Medium Team Final at 2012 European Open

#5
Control

The fifth and final "C" of the *muscles-over-mind* system is Control. All the previous concepts, skill development techniques, and new habits have been leading directly to Control. With all the work you've now done with the mental management tools, it is the easiest concept to understand and incorporate into your daily life and competition days.

There are three levels of control: thought, emotion, and energy. Each one directly impacts the others. This is where the *muscles-over-mind* ideas become a system.

> If you can dream it, you can do it.
> ~Walt Disney

Thought Control

The first two "C's" are Calm and Centered. The primary intent of the techniques and tools in Calm and Centered is to first make you aware of your thoughts and second to shift them toward and into the present moment. The basic skills that we've collected and learned for Calm and Centered also allow you to control your thoughts in competitive and stressful situations.

Emotion Control

With though control, you can work the middle "C" which is Clear Focus. It is only possible to maintain focus on a goal, plan or specific result when you are calm and centered. With Clear Focus, we created a goal plan with detailed steps and a well defined journey toward your dream. This gives you a framework for generating success and managing upsets and disappointments. With focus your efforts are aligned and balanced. It may not have exactly the same gleeful abandonment you had toward your sport in the past, but we guarantee you'll get better results and have more fun with your dog.

Think of it this way....you are much more likely to slip and fall running downhill than you are jogging slowly, steadily up a mountain. The downhill freefall might be fun but there's no control and a high risk of crash and burn. And, unfortunately, it is sometimes your canine partner who takes the brunt of your fall. Controlling your emotions may eliminate the occasional high but the views at the top are truly worth the climb!

Energy Control

With both thought and emotion control, you move onto the fourth "C" which is Confidence. This rather involved concept pulls together and relies on many of the skills necessary in the first three "C's". By maintaining thought and emotion control, you can manage your energy through every situation and competition. You can trap negative thoughts before they start, eliminate self-defeating ideas and fears, and maintain a positive attitude that matches your dog's.

Think of the energy flow when you feel good! You can accomplish anything when you stay on track and have a positive mindset.

Dream Achievement

With thought, emotion, and energy control your dream can easily become your new reality!

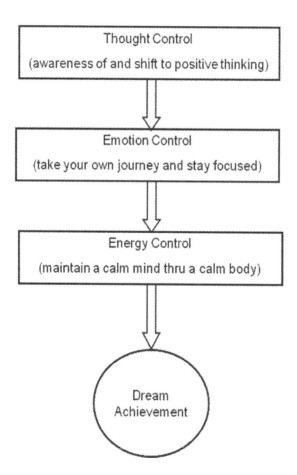

Whimzy – Control in Motion

Jack – Ruler of the Pack

The
Competition Day

A detailed, specific handling or training system is a great step toward success but the system must still be implemented. It must also be usable and maintainable. In this final section, Kathleen and I present how we use all the *muscles-over-mind* concepts and tools at competitions. Our goal with this information is to give you a working plan for competition days. How you use the tools and when will be a very individualized process and it will change as your experience and goals change.

When you are reading them on your coach with one hand lazily scratching your pup's tummy, sport psychology concepts and ideas are common sense and seem perfectly reasonable. When you are competing, it is a completely different story. At a trial, very few of the sports psychology ideas make it beyond the need to potty the dog, check-in, talk with fellow competitors or your coach, get your equipment organized, and get you and your dog warmed up. It was this difficulty that slowed me down for years. Even after reading and studying literally dozens of golf and sport psychology books, I knew I should be calm and should do some breathing exercises but the how, where and when eluded me.

Thankfully, in 2009, I came across Jason Selk's book, *10-Minute Toughness*. He does not just present concepts. Selk explains how to use real techniques and tools and puts them together in a program. He does not tell his readers to be calm. He actually describes how to become calm and when! Furthermore, his 10-minute mental toughness program, which is a mental training program for athletes in any sport, changed the way I was thinking and gave me concrete ideas on how to use the skills I had read about. This was the true beginning of the system within *muscles-over-mind*. Knowing is not the same as being able to do.

There are five elements of the *muscles-over-mind* system that need to be built directly into your competition day. Each uses parts of the five C's and the mental management tools you've now learned.

- Identify Control Points

- Build Routines

- Create a Simulation

- Use your Simulation

- Develop a Mental Management Routine

He who keeps his cool best wins.
~Norman Cousins

Identify Control Points

Through the five "C's", you have a pathway to thought, emotion and energy control. All of these have one thing in common. They are all centered on you. They are all internal to your mind and body. As you work toward control – calm, centered, focused and confident – you need to always be mindful that some elements and events are not controllable. Every competition day will have a few bumps, distractions and rough spots. Some of these will be easy to resolve and forget; others not so much. Where you apply your energy and how you focus your thoughts is as critical as maintaining a calm mind. Kathleen and I counsel each other and our students to identify (quickly) whether an element or event is controllable or uncontrollable. The answer dictates your response.

- Controllable events

- Uncontrollable events

- Focus on the controllable

Controllable events. These are the elements and events that should be given considerable attention. By definition, controllable events let you manage your day and help you maintain a calm, relaxed mind. This is where you begin to incorporate the critical components of the *muscles-over-mind* system, from clothing color selections to rest to nutrition to time management. Mental management begins long before you enter the ring.

Consider the following common activities on trial days....
- dog equipment preparation – articles, dumbbell, leash, treats, crates, etc
- your equipment preparation – clothing, shoes, raingear, umbrella, sunblock, gloves & hat, tent, chairs, coolers, etc
- rest
- food preparation and packing
- water for you and your dog
- directions - knowing where trial is located
- travel - being on-time or early
- check-in at ring
- your own performance

All of the above are directly under your control. You pack your bag, select an outfit, eat well, pack breakfast/lunch, and get enough sleep the day of or before a competition. You are also responsible for knowing where you are going and getting there with plenty of time to potty and walk your dog, get organized, relax and check-in. The time needed for each of these is very dependent on the individual. Kathleen and I, working as a team with one car, can get to a local trial within thirty minutes of our first walkthrough. Many of our students want an hour or more. How much time is not important, what is important is knowing how much time you need and building that into your schedule with conscious planning. Being on time – for you – is under your control.

You are also in control of your performance. At every competition, do the best you can do. The

> *You need to be mindful that some elements of every day are not controllable. Find the ones that are and let go of the others.*

muscles-over-mind system is specifically designed to give you control over your performance and to enjoy your time with your dog. It does not guarantee you a win or even a qualifying score. Focusing on those items that you can control just makes the day happier and the time spent with your furry friend more fun.

It's a dog trial not a battle for world peace.
~ Cindy Schmitt

Uncontrollable events. On the opposite side, there are plenty of events/elements of a trial day that are uncontrollable. These sink many handlers. They fuss and fume all day about situations over which they have no influence or control. The following is a (very short) list of uncontrollable events and elements common to dog events, trials or tests:
- traffic
- parking
- weather
- venue environment: building, arena, field, park, etc
- club equipment
- class size
- ring size and/or location
- crating space
- competition's performance
- judge behavior or calls
- course flow or heeling pattern
- stock (sheep, duck or cattle) behavior
- scheduling conflicts

All of us have been delayed, aggravated, and annoyed on trial days or on the way to evening class. Construction on the highway can throw your whole routine into chaos. Rainy, cold weather can make you rethink taking up Bingo as a hobby! Preparing for rain is fine. Fuming because it is raining – that is a waste of time and energy. There really are only two choices. Put your rain gear on or go home.

On trial days, there is also nothing you can do about the venue once you have entered and then driven there! Check out the competition building or site ahead of time and accept that over the weekend event, you will do your best regardless. If the conditions don't work for you, then you do have control over whether you compete. Both Kathleen and I have pulled our dogs when the rings were excessively muddy. It's just one day of competition while an injury can cost us an entire season. You also obviously have no control over the judge, ring setup, spooky stock, or your competition's performance. We have seen herding trial judges help hold stock or an agility judge adjust a piece of equipment for safety. However, most days everyone just deals with the flighty sheep or runs the course as it is presented. While your fellow competitors are complaining, you can accept the situation, figure out the best way to handle the challenge, and get back on routine.

Attitude is a little thing that makes
a big difference.
~Winston Churchill

Checklists

Make checklist for my stuff, check. Make even longer checklist for the dog's stuff, check. Make checklist for stuff I'll need on the plane, check. Find new checking marker for more satisfied checking, check.

Shoe pair one, shoe pair two, shoe pair three, check. Shirts, check. Backup shirt, check. Coat, check. Running pants, check. Shorts, check. Backup pants, check. Bathroom supplies, check. Double check for toothbrush, check. Socks, underwear, belts, unnecessary accessories just in case, check. Clothing, completed, big check.

Back-on-Track coat, check. Fuzzy show leash, check. Harness, check. Collar, check. Treats, check. Dog food day one, dog food day two, dog food day three, check. Emergency medicines, just in case, check. Hotel crate, check. Show crate, check. Bedding, check. Show tarp, check. Video camera, check. Zillions of poop bags, check. Bedtime biscuits (for dogs), check. Whimzy's bedtime stuffed dragon toy, check. Dog completed, big check. Food and water bowls, still not packed....no check.

Travel documents, check. Phone charger, check. Phone, check. I-pad, check. Camera, check. Travel leash, check. Dog airline carrier, check. Purse, check. Homework that I won't be doing, but makes Mom happy to think I might do, check. Plane supplies, completed, big check.

Triple check for toothbrush, check. Double check all checklists, che...crap ...forgot my PJs. Pack PJs, check. Double check all checklists, chec....crap... forgot the dog bowls. Finally pack dog bowls, check. Double check all checklists, check. Panic that I may have still forgotten something important, check. Prepare to cope with the fact that I forgot something anyway, check.

Quiz Mom to be sure she has credit cards so I can buy whatever I forgot (and more), check and double check.

Agility and Beyond Blog - Kathleen Oswald - December 11, 2013

Focus on the controllable. The bottom line for every activity and situation is to put your efforts and focus on the controllable events and elements of your competition day.

Identify the controllable element/event. Ask yourself all day whether you have control. Literally ask yourself, "Is this something over which I have control?" At the very least, asking and answering the question will put the situation in context. If you have to answer "no", you might not feel better but you will have made the first step back toward a positive mindset.

Work around uncontrollable elements. When you find something over which you have no control, work around it. This is the true power of a positive mental attitude. You can use the negative situation or event to your advantage!

Unexpected aggravations offer opportunities to practice your calming techniques. Unusual venue situations simulate what you'll find at major tournaments. Use the situation to practice your mindset for when you are at larger, more stressful events or tournaments. Missing or forgotten equipment can be handled by buying new from a vendor or borrowing from a friend. I've purchased rain gear, T-shirts, sweatshirts, hats, crates, chairs, lunch, snacks, water and dog treats on more than one occasion or trip. In Germany at the 2010 World Championships, I slipped badly in the practice run so I promptly went outside and bought new Dita running shoes, which had much deeper tread than the shoes I brought. There's very little a positive attitude and a VISA card cannot fix!

Allow extra time. Extra time is a major survival tool against the uncontrollable. A few extra minutes can give you breathing room to reshape your thoughts and regain control of emotions and then your energy. Upsets happen but you do not need to remain upset. Allow extra time to reorganize, redirect, go shopping, or just plain figure something else out. It is also important to add even more time into your routines when you are not "local." Everyone has a pattern for trial days and these patterns make assumptions. When you are trialing locally, you know where to get coffee, where to park, traffic patterns, ring setups, etc. When you are on the road or at a big tournament, make sure you adjust your schedules to allow for disruptions and to find workable solutions for the inevitable uncontrollable situations.

Let it go. Sometimes the only defense against uncontrollable situations is to simply "let it go!" Accept – as quickly as possible – that the event is outside your control and move on. If necessary, you may need to verbalize this sentiment to yourself. Take time to mentally move yourself beyond the disturbing element and get into a positive, energizing mental place. You may also have to walk away from friends and/or training partners if they are stuck on a negative. Be wary of too many negative conversations!

Happiness doesn't depend on any external conditions, it is governed by our mental attitude.
~ Dale Carnegie

Build Routines

One of the key habits of successful competitors, in any sport, is their ability to create and maintain a consistent routine. As a competitor, a detailed routine is a necessity. No matter what happens or when, you always have a pattern to go to. Remember your mind is wired for habitual behavior. It likes patterns! A competition routine is a series of deliberate "good habits." By creating and maintaining a routine you give your mind an anchor against disruptions. Even at well run local trials, you will inevitably encounter delays and minor aggravations. Equipment breaks. Conflicts develop between rings. Competitors get stressed or just have a bad attitude/behavior. Judges get sick or have travel conflicts. Being in your routine, especially when it's flexible, provides a buffer against all these typical distractions and anything else that disrupts the day. And, when you go to larger events or tournaments, where there are even more unknowns and unexpected situations, your routine will keep you grounded and guide you back to calm and relaxed.

Within competitive dog events, there are multiple places for routines. Each provides unique advantages for the successful competitor:

- Pre-competition routine

- Mini-routines

- Post-competition routine

Patience is not simply the ability to wait – it's how we behave while we're waiting.
~Joyce Meyer

Pre-competition routine. For best results, your pre-competition routine should be created (not just evolved) and it should always be the same. And, as much as possible, it should be the same for all the dogs that you trial. Variations allow mistakes. Once your routine is created, you should use it everywhere. Using the same routine at matches, local trials, and major tournaments reduces stress and keeps you focused. Settling into a familiar routine, even while trialing at Nationals or the Invitational, is calming to your mind. Nerves get pushed back a bit by the sense of control. In this way, a competition routine can keep even big competitions small!

Over the years, my routine has become very simple, as has Kathleen's. I put on my running shoes, do a few simple leg warm-up exercises, find the video camera, get out treats, and then get the dog for a quick potty and warm-up walk. As I approach the car or crate, I repeat: shoes, warm-up, camera, treats and dog. For a nosework trial, I might not switch shoes and at a herding trial I might put on boots but the basic elements of the routine – regardless of which sport or competition level – are the same.

When creating your pre-competition routine, consider the following guidelines…

Keep is simple. A competition routine should be natural and repeatable. Simple should be a major goal when you create your routine. If you are working a short list, you can relax and move through the activities easily. If the list is long or complex, you may find yourself working the routine. None of your routines should add stress! A good routine is just a good habit - easy and mechanical. Routines relax your mind since they are familiar. When you are already in a stressful situation, you can get an even bigger benefit from a simple routine.

When you settle into a familiar routine, you calm your mind and the ensuing sense of control soothes twitchy nerves.

Write it down. With a short, simple list of activities, you can write them down. Not only does this make the competitive routine real, but it gives you time to reflect on each activity. Is it necessary or something you just do? Does the order of activities make sense or are you duplicating effort? Are you giving yourself adequate time to prepare before you start working with your dog? Are there superstitious actions on the list? Many competitive athletes have a few superstitions and frequently these competitors use the superstitious action as a settling point, very much like a personal centering trigger. There is nothing wrong with superstitious actions or behaviors so long as they are manageable and you can put them in your routine.

Keep it short. A written routine also lets you do a time check. Does your routine take five minutes or forty-five minutes? A simple routine should be relatively short, more like five to ten minutes than forty. My routine takes less than five minutes. With your routine set with a known timeframe, you will also know when to start no matter where you are competing.

Sometimes it may also be necessary, due to one of those pesky uncontrollable events, to shorten or compress your routine. Consider – before it's required - where to trim or cut when needed.

Prevent ritualizing. A routine is not a ritual. If you find yourself religiously doing the same behaviors in the exact same order, then your routine has shifted from a good habit to a ritual. For example, if one of your actions is to switch to competition shoes and you typically put the right shoe on before the left, then you are fine. However, if one day you put on the left first and find yourself taking it off to put the right one on first....you have created a ritual! There is a fine line behind good habits and rituals. Good habits settle the mind and keep you flexible, which let you get critical tasks done - even with distractions and nerves – in a timely fashion. Rituals require more mental energy and reduce flexibility, which adds stress.

Check your energy state. When creating a routine, add an activity to check your mental state. My energy state check is built into the leg warm-up exercises. If I am cold or tired, I do a few more or cycle through the exercises twice. If I am charged up, then I add a few full body stretches to remove tension and settle down. Kathleen does her mental check during the potty and warm-up walk. If she's tired, she walks faster to get energy. If she's wired, she deliberately slows down and strolls. A quick energy-level check also works as a reminder to check your breathing and begin using your mental management skills.

Become a competitor. When you begin your competition routine, you become a competitor. You are no longer a friend, spectator, trainer or coach. You are the competitor. Let others' issues fade as you move through your routine. This is particularly important if you bring family or have students at a trial. With a set routine, you can gently but firmly let others know that you need to focus for a short time on yourself and your dog. This is a critical mental shift.

> To change a habit, make a conscious decision,
> then act out the new behavior.
> ~ Maxwell Maltz

Mini-routines. There are also mini-routines that many competitors use within or during an event. For example, in agility you may create and maintain a specific routine for your dog at the warm-up jump. Both Kathleen and I have several exercises that we do with the dogs to be sure our handling signals are in-sync with the dog and that the dog's muscles are warmed up appropriately. In obedience, you may find mini-routines in several places. One of the most common is a short routine to keep the dog's attention before entering the ring. Many successful obedience handlers also have a specific pattern when moving between exercises.

Mini-routines should also follow all of the guidelines suggested for the pre-competition routine.

Post-competition routine. The last routine is the one most often skipped. Both you and your dog will benefit from a post-competition routine. As you exit the ring or field and celebrate with your dog for his wonderful efforts, you should eventually settle into another short routine. Take time to warm down and stretch your dog and give yourself a few moments to evaluate your performance. This is the point to do a quick mental review of what just happened.

A post-competition review can answer some critical questions before the feeling of the performance fades, gets rationalized, or is blurred by others comments. Ask yourself a few good questions. Did you do what you planned? If not, where did you vary and why? Did you use your mental management techniques? Were they effective? What do you need to improve? Did you work your routines? Did they work as expected? What went perfectly and needs to be reviewed for confidence building?

Create a Simulation

One of the biggest advantages in the *muscles-over-mind* system is the mental control needed to create and effectively use mental imagery. Your mind is extremely powerful. A quiet mind can do amazing things and one of these is a full competition simulation.

A simulation is a complete, highly detailed mental run thru of a training set or competitive event – be it a twenty-two second agility run or a ten minute Utility test. A mind that is jumpy, distracted or stressed cannot maintain the focus needed for a valuable simulation - even a short one. The five "C's" are all designed to get your mind into the zone and keep it there. Remember, when your left-brain (the thinking, analytical side) is quiet and the right brain is working with your body, optimal performances can occur and they can be in your mind before they are real.

Effective simulations are just one more benefit of being calm and relaxed. A mental simulation is a practice run in your mind. Think about the success possible when you run-thru an obedience exercise, rally routine, or agility course two or three or four times before you even get your dog out of the car! This is true whether the run is real or in your mind.

Kathleen and I use the term simulation versus visualization on purpose. Visualization implies sight only. A simulation uses all your senses and, in some cases, your entire body.

When you are at a competition, a detailed simulation can create your entire event in your mind. Simulations can also be used in training or practice. They let you learn new skills quickly and let you perfect cues and signals without wearing out or confusing your dog. Simulations can be used anywhere - and everywhere - in your training and competitions. Once you have developed the skill of creating simulations, you will find lots of ways to use them – both in agility and in life. A simulation is truly your mind unleashed!

For the *muscles-over-mind* system, we will focus on using simulations in competition. Although mental imagery is also a powerful training tool, it is a bit beyond the scope of this book. For competition simulations, there are several critical skills to explore to help you develop strong simulation techniques. The key theme behind each component is details. The fine points make the simulation real to your mind. Without specifics, your mind will run a simulation that is hazy and vague and it will not match your actual experience. Adding details requires practice. And, like all competitive tools, it is important to begin with simple exercises and work toward complex. Within each section, we present practice drills and ideas on how to develop the skill and technique. Be patient. Some skills will be easy and natural; others will take time to establish. You will, however, get immediate benefits out of each session.

The basic components of a simulation are:

- Identify the setting

- Create a starting/ending point

- Select a reference point

- Develop visualization

- Add a soundtrack

- Incorporate the physical feelings

- Identify your emotions

Always continue the climb. It is possible for you to do whatever you choose, if you first get to know who you are and are willing to work with the power that is greater than ourselves to do it.
~ Ella Wilcox

Identify the setting. For a competition simulation, this part is relatively easy to define. When you are physically at an event, you know what the site looks like and what ring, field or building your event is in. When you begin collecting details for your simulation, start on the outer edges and move slowly and deliberately into the competition area.

Start by taking note of the surrounding area including the stands, bleachers or seating areas. Look at where the stewards, gate manager or ring crew is located. Find the entrance and exit points. For herding events, there are lots of critical details with regards to stock handling, gate positions and pressure points that should be noted. In agility, obedience and rally, you should study the ring gating and edges. Really look at what is immediately outside the ring and on the walls, fences or gating. Add details thoughtfully and precisely as you move through the environment. Engage all your senses. Use your eyes first but you should also close them and let yourself absorb the sounds and smells of the area. This is good place to use the complete breath exercise. It allows you to focus on deep breaths and just notice your environment.

From the surrounding and edges, move your senses into the competition ring or field. Take note of the surface. What does it look like? How does it feel when you touch it or walk/run on it? Pay attention to the specifics such as color, painted lines or decorations, seams, or the composition of the dirt or grass. Is it clumpy and bumpy or slippery? Are there areas to avoid? Check the equipment – whatever is appropriate for you sport – and notice its location. Make a mental map of the competition area. You need to be able to locate all the personnel, equipment, gates, tables, stock, pens, etc in the ring. Pay close attention to colors and shapes. These exact details are what your mind needs for a strong simulation.

Building the environment or scene for your simulation requires practice. We suggest that our students practice this skill by using a familiar site first and then move into practice and competition areas.

Familiar room. Select a room or small area with which you are very familiar. This can be your cubicle, private office, family or living room. Start at a doorway and find all the furniture, rugs and decorations. Notice all the colors, textures and smells. See the pattern on the floor, drapes and furniture. Use your mind to pick up and look at your pictures, statutes, trophies, etc. Once you have the room set, let your mind walk through the room. Mentally turn on the computer, television or stereo and sit on a chair or couch. What can you see when sitting? Feel the room temperature. Is it warm or cold? If the room feels hazy or you cannot get details firm in your mind, go to the edge of the room and study it. Add details and try again.

Training location. Use your regular or local training site first. Start on the outside and work toward the front door or gate. Notice how the building is organized. Pick out the doors, windows, office, bathroom, equipment storage, and/or crating. Look at and feel the floor surface as you move across it. Did you picture the building/field empty or with a class? Turn slowly like you are videotaping the area and look at the details on each wall. Move your eyes from the ceiling to the floor and truly look at the walls. It is also important to take a minute to close your eyes. Let your mind absorb the smells and sounds and temperature. Again, if the scene in your mind is hazy, take a few minutes the next time you are there to absorb details and try again.

Competition site. Your first job at the competition will be to sit quietly and calm your mind. Use your breathing exercises to get into a relaxed state. You will also want to be in the vicinity of the competition area so you can feel and check details as you build the environment. As always, start on the outer edge and build into the center of the competition ring/field. Create a detailed scene in your mind starting with your entry point. At this point, you do not need to put in your performance. Just picture and feel the trial environment with all its sights, sounds and smells. With practice, you will

> **Map the Room**
>
> If you cannot get a clear mental picture of the area or room, grab some paper and try sketching the entire space. Drawing will engage the right-side of your brain, which may have a better sense of shapes, patterns and colors than your left-side.

notice and absorb details quicker and will be able to incorporate specifics quickly and easily.

Creating a scene gets a little more involved when you are simulating an event at a site that you have not been to yet or are not allowed into until the event begins. When this happens, select the closest building or site that you do know and modify the scene with information, pictures or video of the real site. In order to get details before you travel, try searching YouTube or the Internet for videos of other competitions/events that were held at the site in the past.

> Clarity affords focus.
> ~Thomas Leonard

Create a staring/ending point. Every simulation must have a detailed, specific start and end. Pick an action to begin the simulation. For example, you can start your simulation of a competition when you enter the ring or when you remove your dog's leash or when the judge says "go." It is okay to test different start points but identify a specific point to anchor the simulation. You must also select a distinct end to the simulation. In AKC agility or obedience, we always tell our students to end the competition simulation with putting their dog's leash on! For herding simulations, you might end with the sheep successfully in the exhaust chute or penned. Again, it doesn't matter too much where you end so long as it is predefined.

The end point of a simulation is particularly important for mental focus. It is very easy while inside a simulation to get sidetracked or distracted. With an exact end point, you can refocus your mind and work thru the entire exercise, test or course. Once thru to the end, you can go back and examine what distracted you. It is critical, however, that you get through the entire simulation every time you start. This often requires significant mental focus.

In order to practice this skill, we have our students work thru a few simple tasks and then do a training exercise before trying to simulate an entire competition event.

Simple task. Select a simple task like starting your car, brushing your teeth or tying your shoe. Mentally run through the basics of the task to select a start point, accomplish the task, and then distinctly end it. You should also identify your setting. For example, you may start a simulation on tying your shoe with picking the shoe up off the floor or off a shelf in your closet or you may start with it in your hand while sitting on a bench or chair or you may start with the shoe already on your foot. Again, it doesn't matter at what point you begin the simulation but you must have a setting defined and the start point must be clear-cut. For an ending, you can select tugging the knot tight or letting go of the bow or standing up. Any point is fine so long as you have an ending that is precise. Other simple simulations, like laying out utility articles, grooming your dog, completing an entry form, or baking dog treats will give you practice at identifying starting/end points.

Training exercise. Once you have worked through a few simple tasks, try running through a short training exercise. For your first couple simulations, select something simple like entering the ring, weaves from a table, or a recall to heel. Alternately, you can select a handling move like an outrun, rally turn, or an agility front/rear cross.

The only objective of the exercise is to identify a specific start and end point for each simulation.

Competition event. After you have gained proficiency at selecting logical, repeatable start and end points, try simulating a competitive event or routine that is less than sixty seconds. You can steadily build up to longer simulations should your sport require them. While developing this skill, it is not necessary to do the whole simulation. You are simply gaining practice at defining start and end points. Be mindful of the length of time between your start and end. As simulations get longer, their degree of difficulty rises exponentially! Maintaining focus on one task for thirty or sixty seconds is doable. Maintaining focus for ten minutes is extremely difficult until you've had lots of practice.

Start where you are. Use what you have.
Do what you can.
~Arthur Ashe

Select a reference point. Simulations are always run from a specific perspective or viewpoint. There are two reference points: internal and external. Neither is right or wrong. They're just different. Both reference points have advantages and both are necessary skills. The two perspectives engage your mind in different ways. You may find that one is more instinctive and comfortable than the other. If so, actively work on building the other.

Internal. Think of a video camera. With a simulation run with an internal reference point, you are doing the videoing. Picture holding the camera in front of you or having it attached to a hat that you wear on your head. The perspective of the film is from you. It is what you see and feel as you move around the field or ring, give your signals, and interact with your dog. With an internal perspective, you can feel your motions and see the real time event from within yourself. This lets you focus on your signals, motions and your dog's responses.

External. With a simulation run from an external reference point, the video camera is in someone else's hand. You see your whole body and your dog's moving together. This is the perspective of a television show or movie. With an external perspective, you can see and hear the whole picture. This lets you focus on the venue conditions, feeling of the surface, sounds and the location of stock, equipment, judges, ring crew and spectators. If you need help developing this perspective, you can video yourself performing short exercise with your dog and then immediately watch the video. With obedience or rally or freestyle, you can perform in front of a mirror and actively watch yourself complete the exercise.

As with the first two skills, it is important to practice running simulations with different perspectives. Begin the following simulations with whatever reference point is most comfortable for you. Once you have run it thru with your "natural" perspective, run the simulation again with the other reference point. These are just a few suggestions for practicing with different reference points. As you gain experience, it will be important to find other tasks to practice reference point simulations.

Setup a dog crate. This task is familiar, simple and has a relatively short duration. Your first task is to identify where you are and what the start and end points are. With an internal reference point, you should see the crate in your hands and feel all the motions needed to complete the setup. With an external reference point, you should see your whole body and the crate as it is setup.

Drive to work. This task is familiar, requires that you pay attention to more details, and has a longer duration. There is a significant jump in difficulty with this task since there are so many details. In order to remain focused, we suggest you key in on just a few details and add specifics in layers. For example, on your first attempt, drive to work identifying only the major intersections, such as those that have stop signs or stoplights. On your second simulation attempt, identify the intersections and the cross streets. On your third simulation attempt, add more details, such as topography (hills and valleys), traffic, stores, gas stations, schools, firehouses, and hospitals, to the cross streets and intersections. This mental map building method helps our students improve the quality of their simulations. Once you have run thru the process of building a detailed simulation with your "natural" perspective, complete the same process again with the other reference point.

When you are at a trial, do the simulation with whichever reference point is more comfortable and then try the opposite. Learning to use both reference points for a simulation can take time, so be patient and practice as much as possible.

None but ourselves can free our minds.
~Bob Marley

Develop visualization. For humans, our primary sense is sight so a large part of your simulation will be based on visualization. It is important to keep the setting, start and end points, and reference point in mind when you begin to add visual details. There are several tools you can use to get your mind to add visual details.

Identify colors. Go through your simulation and pick out specific colors. Finding specific colors or patterns improves the reality of the simulation ten-fold. For example, in agility picture the equipment in full color from the jumps to the contacts to the weave poles. Let your mind pick out the color of the jumps where your dog is turning and the yellow zone at the end of the contact equipment. In herding, put in details for the sheep – breed, unique markings, size, coat texture, etc. For nosework, picture the inside space with real objects and equipment. For other elements, picture not only the color of the cars but the make and model (i.e., size & shape) and a real outdoor area. For rally, see the holders and signs in color.

Measure distance and space. Go through your simulation and identify the size of the equipment, venue and surrounding. Does the space look cramped or spacious? This can be a feeling but you should also be able to add the visual detail to identify why. Measure the space and distances between equipment and/or gates in your mind. While developing spatial distances, you may need to physically measure the space a few times to improve your mental imagery.

Seek a clear image. We often "see" without focus. Your goal in adding visualizations to your simulation is to get an image that is clear and well defined. Let your mind develop an image that is precise. When you picture an object in the ring, add lots of details, like color, shape, size, lettering, etc. Developing the precision needed for a visualization that your mind feels as real can take time. This is the way an artist sees the world. They don't see a tree. They see a shape, shadows, light, individual branches and leaves. As with scene creation, you may find it helpful to draw the objects for awhile. Drawing loosens the hold your left side has on your thinking and creates more interaction with the right where many of these details are easier to visualize.

See the dog. See the eyes. See the intention.

This skill alone can be a major advantage. It often takes years to build the skills of a professional handler/trainer. Working your visualization skill for precision can shave serious time off this learning curve. When training their dog, novice handlers see a dog in motion. An experienced trainer/handler sees the dog's body – legs, eyes, head, tail – as individual components. A professional trainer/handler sees the dog's intention to move its head, leg, body and eyes. The precision of their focus allows the professional to react much faster than the beginner. Thus, they can communicate with the dog quickly and clearly. Your goal with visualization is to develop the focus of a professional handler/trainer from your couch or office chair!

Use slow motion. When adding details to your simulation, you need to slow your eyes down and concentrate on the specifics. Don't just see. Look! Look for shapes, colors, sizes, distances, spaces, shadows, lights, etc. The process of looking vs seeing is sometimes aided by doing your scan in deliberate slow motion. If it takes you ten seconds to scan a wall, then take sixty or ninety seconds. If you lose focus and start thinking, just gently return your focus to the space, motion, or action and resume picking out details. Slow motion does not mean half speed. It means so slow your left-brain becomes desperate to jump to another activity! By moving your eyes slowly through an area, action, or event, you give your brain a chance to catch-up and absorb more information. A slow motion run thru drives your awareness to a different level. In slow motion, you will notice details that your mind did not see at regular speed. Remember that minutiae equals a real simulation!

The only creatures that are evolved enough to convey pure love are dogs and infants.
~Johnny Depp

Add a soundtrack. In order to create a simulation that your brain feels as real, you must also add a soundtrack. Since hearing is not our dominant sense, you may have to work to add noises and sounds. Your background experience will vastly alter your skill with this exercise. Anyone with music or videography training will find this task significantly easier. In order to get our students started with a soundtrack for their simulations, we suggest focusing on three distinct areas: background noise, judge's voice and their own voice.

Background noise. At a competition site, you can begin your soundtrack by absorbing the sounds of the venue or building while you are working on the setting. Simply close your eyes and listen. There may be a steady rumble of voices from the bleachers or the room may be shockingly silent. After years of noisy, loud agility competitions, I find the relative silence of obedience competitions unnerving. No matter what your sport, the sounds of an outdoor trial will be significantly different than an indoor event. You may also have to adjust your soundtrack as the spectator crowd swells and shrinks throughout the day.

Next add the sounds of your motion and your dog's motion. Determine what sounds you hear when you are heeling through a figure-eight exercise or running beside your dog in the weaves. Pay attention to the difference in sound when you are moving slow or fast. With agility you can easily identify the distinct noises your dog makes as he lands a jump, barrels thru a tunnel, runs the dog walk, or climbs the A-frame. Each sport has a unique soundtrack and your dog's noise will be distinct. If you are working with multiple dogs, pay particular attention to the different noises each one makes. It will help you remain focused on the individual dog as you run a simulation.

Judge's voice. Depending on the sport, the judge's voice is a critical component. For agility, rally, herding and hunt tests, the competitor's interaction with the judge is minimal. In obedience, however, the judge is an integral part of the competition. When you are running a simulation, use a real judge's voice. Identify the voice as male or female and then further differentiate the volume, tone and breathiness. Is the judge's voice gentle or commanding? It is also important to hear the judge so you can select the specific command. With repetition, judges frequently drop inflections or over emphasize, either of which can make the speech pattern sound funny or odd. These are the details that you need to incorporate into your simulations.

Your voice. Verbal commands are integral to all dog sports. Whether you are whispering, shouting or whistling, your verbal communication with your dog is a critical component. Dogs obviously hear better than we do and they pickup on variations in voice quality and tone much more than we want them to! As such, adding your verbal commands to your simulation is very important. When did you speak? How loud? What word or words did you use? Identify the actual word or phrase and when you used it. As always, your goal is precise details.

You don't need anybody to tell you who you are or what you are. You are what you are!
~John Lennon

Incorporate a physical feeling. Engage your body in the simulation. This is where you actually feel the motion and speed of your event or activity. Connecting your mind and body is a critical component of simulation skills. As you mentally execute your simulation, your mind should feel your fingers, hands, arms, hips, legs, feet, head and eyes as you execute your routine. The areas of your brain that control these motions will actually activate if your simulation has enough details. This is the biggest benefit of a simulation. Your mind will truly be practicing even though your body is mostly stationary.

There are several ways to enhance the physical feeling of a simulation.

If you are doing a brand new course, test, or exercise, work through your routine with all the motions. Once you have it down, stop and do a mental simulation. Repeat this pattern of motion-simulation at least two more times. Alternating a real action with a simulation lets both your body and mind work on memorizing perfection. Also try to do at least one simulation with an internal and one with an external reference point.

If you know the course or exercise, do a mental simulation first. This will force you to select precise details and will engage your mind. After the mental simulation, do an actual run-thru in either full scale or small scale making sure to do all the physical motions. Repeat this pattern of simulation-motion at least two more times. So, three complete cycles. The benefit of engaging your mind and body is tremendous. You will sharpen your skills and will go into the ring having practiced multiple times.

Some people want it to happen, some wish it would happen, others make it happen.
~ Michael Jordan

Identify your emotions. The final component for your simulation is to consider how you feel. Excitement changes how you move and react. Running a simulation assuming that you are couch-calm might be comfortable but it is not real. Let your emotions flow into the simulation. They need to be part of the simulation from beginning to end. Think for a moment about how you'll feel at the start and at the end. Are you relaxed and calm or nervous and excited?

An easy way to trigger your emotions is to use the setting of the event to build a true feeling. Let your emotions flow as you create the scene in your mind. See and feel the spectators watching ringside or from the bleachers. Notice the tension and stress of your fellow competitors waiting to go in the ring. Follow the excitement or disappointment of competitors who've already been in. All of these emotions will be around you every time you compete and they will affect you also. When you are waiting for your turn, do you want to talk or sit quietly? Do you pet your dog or keep them in a quiet down? Your emotions can change not only the feeling of the simulation, but what you put in your simulation. If you are nervous and erratic while waiting, then make sure you put your breathing exercises, key phrase repetition and centering trigger in your simulation!

Use your Simulation

Once you know how to build a solid simulation, you will find infinite uses both in and out of world of dog sports. You can run simulations to smooth out a difficult discussion with an employee, channel calmness during a dentist visit, or prep for a job interview. Any situation or event can be simulated and it's all great practice for your competition skills too. Our primary focus is on how to use a simulation when you are competing, so a few simple guidelines for using simulations are:

Vary the speed. Try to run the simulation in your mind at a normal speed. If necessary, get out a stopwatch and actually time your simulation. It should be relatively close to the actual event. This is also an excellent proof to know that you've added the appropriate level of detail. Once you've mastered the normal speed simulation, run your simulation in slow motion or in hyper-speed. In slow motion, you have time to focus on different sensations and actions. It will also force you to be extremely precise. Remember, slow motion does not mean half speed. It means s........l........o........w. In hyper-speed, you will be forced to change your rhythm and timing. Frequently, this is how our students feel when actually in a competition! Rushing on purpose can be a valuable proof for your mind.

Work from start to finish. Whenever you run thru a simulation, your mind will wander or pickup a new detail. Unless the new information drastically changes your mental state or the foundation of the simulation, ignore the new detail and keep going to the end. The best part of mental simulations is that they're easily repeatable. You can always go back to your simulation template, make the change, and rerun the simulation.

Be perfect. Your mental simulation should be mistake free. If you make a mistake or encounter a problem, stop and rewind a bit. Replay over the mistake and make it perfect. Only when it's perfect should you then continue to the end. Every simulation should be as close to perfect as possible. There is absolutely no benefit to mentally reviewing mistakes! Remember your mind will happily repeat what you teach it. This is critical when you are playing around in your head. Make sure you have a solid plan or pattern before you begin running a mental simulation. What you think is what you'll get in the ring. Practice perfect at all times.

Check your partner. When you are running multiple dogs, it is important to maintain focus on a specific dog through the entire simulation. It is easy to start with one dog and then realize you've switched dogs right in the middle of the simulation! This is definitely an occurrence where you should halt the simulation and reset. Figure out where you "switched" dogs and figure out why. It may be that the movement, signal, or motion fit better with one dog or it may just be a comfort level. Either way rerun the simulation with your focus on the correct dog.

Modify negative thoughts or emotions. Another excellent use of simulations is to work through negative thoughts and emotions. You can give your mind a template for shifting from negative to positive by running simulations. No one is happy and worry free all the time. We all have disappointments, negative events, and ugly interactions that must be dealt with. The trick to being positive is to move quickly away from the negative. At competitive events, these negative situations can ruin a day. Spend some time building a simulation with a negative event or conversation and mentally practice letting go of it and moving into a positive state. Remember, your mind likes patterns and is programmed to use habits. Good habits can be simulated just as easily as bad.

Vitality shows in not only the ability to persist but the ability to start over.
~F. Scott Fitzgerald

Develop a Mental Management Routine

This is the crux of the whole process. You now have all the tools to truly use mental management techniques at a competition. Your goal is to manage your mental state in competition, stay positively focused, and be the same partner for your dog at every event. You now know how to run an effective, success-oriented simulation and you can calm and relax your mind with the mental management tools from the five C's of success.

With all these skills and techniques, you can build a highly successful competition routine for mental management. Both Kathleen and I use this routine at every agility competition for every run. It completes the link between mind and body and settles the mind in just a few minutes. Our competition routine is based on the concepts by Jason Selk in *10 Minute Mental Management Training*. In the book, he recommends a daily regime of a10 minute mental training session. While the practice of mental training is excellent and we do incorporate it into our training schedules, we've found that mental management control at the competition is just as powerful. Basically, we swapped out the middle. Where Selk recommends reviewing a competition or highlight reel of best movements as the simulation, we encourage our students to simulate their actual trial or test while at the event.

There are five simple activities to the mental management routine. The length of the routine is dependent on the length of your typical competition. For agility where an entire course is run in under thirty seconds, the routine can be done in two minutes or less. For obedience where a utility test takes about ten minutes, then the routine may take fifteen minutes to complete. The components of the mental management routine are:

- Calm breathing

- State your key phrase

- Run a simulation

- State your confidence affirmation

- Calm breathing

Calm breathing. In order to get a calm relaxed mind that can settle into focus on a simulation, you are going to use several cycles of the 4-7-8 breathing exercise. Do two cycles and if you are not completely relaxed, then do three. If you are not relaxed after three cycles, then you are too tense to begin a mental management routine. We recommend that our students take a walk or run through a full body stretch to relax the body. Try the 4-7-8 breathing exercises again after walking or stretching.

State your key phrase. As always, once you are calm, we want to focus your mind immediately. State your key phrase. You can say it in your head or whisper it to yourself. Your key phrase sets your mind's focus point. It also helps maintain your mind in the present state. If you are running multiple events, like Jumpers and Standard in agility or Open and Utility in obedience, be sure to state the key phrase that you've selected for that event.

Run a simulation. With your mind both calm and focused, you want to do a full simulation. Do the simulation with whatever reference point (internal or external) you are most comfortable. If both work well for you, then you can do two simulations, one from each reference point. You can repeat the simulations for confidence and technical excellence.

Over the years, Kathleen and I have incorporated a few variations on the single simulation. We both find that an internal simulation is our dominant perspective but we begin this task with an external simulation, which lets us check flow lines and overall positioning on the agility course. Mentally running with an external perspective often tells us whether the distance and speed built into out handling plan is correct and/or doable. Once that is complete, an internal simulation is an excellent way to proof the technical aspect of an agility run. With an internal reference point, you can see, feel and hear all your hand, body, and verbal cues. There are also times when we will run the internal simulation more than once to perfect the timing of cues and handling moves. Thus, the run a simulation task may take two or three loops to be complete. However, we've now "run" the course three times!

State your confidence affirmation. A confidence affirmation gets your mind into a positive mindset. It is also a reminder to execute your class, run, or test with confidence. You can say the affirmation in your head or you can whisper it to yourself. Either way, take a moment to absorb the power of the affirmation and let your mind truly believe. This is particularly important when you are close to competing, where fear, doubt, and anxiety want to nudge their way into your psyche.

Calm breathing. After running one or more competition simulations and stating a powerful confidence affirmation, your energy level will be high. In order to complete your mental management routine, you want to return to a calm relaxed state. Thus, you will finish the routine with several cycles of the 4-7-8 breathing exercise. Do two cycles and if you are not completely relaxed, then do three.

What we achieve inwardly will change our outer reality.
~Plutarch

As you work with your mental management routine, you will need to adjust and modify the timing of when to do the full routine. It is extremely important that you not feel rushed. Earlier in the day is much better than rushing through it minutes before you are to enter the ring. A solid routine will become instinctive and very settling since it gives your conscious mind a task. With this in mind, you may find it useful to run thru the routine as you wait in line. Multiple repetitions of your mental management routine cannot hurt your performance!

Just be sure to incorporate the time needed for your mental prep routine into your pre-competition routine. Both Kathleen and I do our mental prep before we get our dog. Once you are mentally prepared, go get your dog and go have fun!

Conclusion

A last word.....while building the *muscles-over-mind* system we frequently came across a new idea or technique - sometimes in conversation with other competitors, sometimes from a new sport psychology website or book, sometimes just a new thought. We always take time to explore the new idea(s) and encourage you to do the same. Mental management is not an exclusive system or training methodology. It is a set of comprehensive tools and techniques. As such, it is always evolving.

Sometimes we found the new concept was useful and put it into our system, sometimes not. Now that you've been exposed to many of the concepts of sports psychology and are looking to incorporate more mental management techniques into your competition day, we are sure you too will find new ideas all around you. An "Ah Ha!" moment may come from an article, a conversation, a web post, a commercial, or a book but it will happen. We cannot encourage you enough to explore fully every "Ah Ha!" moment.

We also sincerely hope that you now a have solid foundation with which to create and maintain your own mental management system. Our wish is that you can incorporate new ideas and techniques as you find them and add them to your competition routines for continued success and fun with your dog.

Whimzy – USDAA Regional Steeplechase Finals

About Diane

After a decade or so of training dressage horses, Diane switched to training dogs. It was in 1992 that she began training her first obedience dog, a little Lhasa named Sandy. In between work as a business analyst and having two children, Diane trained Sandy to complete their AKC CD, CDX, and UD and attended two Pupperoni Eastern Regionals. With their obedience titles complete, Sandy and Diane took up agility for fun and Diane was soon hooked. Her first Border collie, Kayla, earned her CD and CDX quickly so they could focus on agility. Kayla earned her AKC novice agility title in April of 1999 and completed both excellent titles eighteen months later, qualifying for the 2002 Agility Nationals where they finished 30th. Kayla earned her MACH later that year and completed her UD a year later. She then shifted to herding. With Kayla retired from agility and happily chasing ducks around the backyard, Diane got her first sheltie, whom the kids named Demon.

The little sable sheltie was a surprise birthday present from Diane's husband, Richard. After a few years of training hiccups and bobbles, they quickly became a competitive force in the 16" division on the East coast. In 2008, they finished 3rd at the AKC Nationals and in 2010 they won a spot on the AKC World Team heading to Germany. With two clean rounds, they finished a solid 15th in Individual medium dogs in their first international completion. In 2012, they competed in Sweden at the European Open where they were both Individual and Team finalists. In 2013, they again won a spot on the AKC International Team. At the European Open in Belgium, Demon and Diane put down a clean round in the medium dog Team Finals helping USA1 - Medium finish 7th. Demon retired from agility after Belgium and moved onto doing nosework.

Diane is now working with her second Border collie, Kenzie. This young team has moved steadily through and into a new handling system and is now qualified and ready for the 2014 AKC Nationals and tryouts for the European Open. Diane is also training with two young shelties, Bazinga and Bizzy, for agility, obedience, rally and nosework.

Working with many different breeds in multiple dog sports has allowed Diane to develop her skills as a competitor and to share this knowledge with her students. She understands how to have fun with her dogs while competing at the highest levels.

About Kathleen

Kathleen started her agility career with Diane's second Lhasa, Jack. The two built a solid relationship and completed several AKC agility titles. Training and competing with a capricious Lhasa taught Kathleen how to handle any situation with flexibility and grace. When her first sheltie, Jenna, joined the family, the two quickly earned titles in both AKC and USDAA agility. Kathleen and Jenna qualified for and attended their first AKC World Team Tryouts in 2010. After two more years of successful Nationals and Tryouts, they were invited to join the 2012 European Open team that competed in Sweden. In 2013, Jenna and Kathleen made Finals at the AKC Nationals and went on to Tryouts to win a spot on the AKC International Team. At the European Open in Belgium, they qualified for the Individual Small Dog finals and ended up as the highest rank USA Small Dog. At seventeen, Kathleen was the youngest handler to represent the USA in international competition.

Kathleen's second sheltie, Whimzy, was selected as an alternate for the AKC International Team in 2013. In 2014, Kathleen and Whimzy were selected for the AKC World Championship team that will compete in Luxembourg in September.

Besides her own shelties, Kathleen trains and competes with a wide variety of dogs in agility from Labradors to poodles to Dobermans. At the 2013 AKC Nationals, she and Nikki (a friend's Doberman) put down three clean rounds to qualify for the Finals where they put down another clean round to finish 2nd in the 20" Preferred class.

As the co-pilot for her mother's quest to be on the AKC World Team in 2010 and then on her own AKC World Team journey in 2014, Kathleen learned the benefits of mental management techniques early. She uses the tools and techniques explained in *The Top Dog Advantage* every time she goes to the start line. For her, mental management is just a normal aspect of a trial day and it allows her to enjoy every moment of competing with her dogs.

Acknowledgements

For my guinea pig group, who were always willing to try new tools and listened while I muttered my way through new concepts, we sincerely thank you, specifically Cindy Schmitt, Laurie Bowen, Lori Brady, Eleanor Campbell, Marie Potts, and, of course, our agility students at Top Dog and Princeton. This thank you list must also include our training partners Rose Savkov and Jeri Prekop.

Thank you to our fellow trainers and competitors at Top Dog, particularly Betsy Scapicchio, who always encouraged me and her other students to strive for excellence, and Petra Ford, who sets that bar really high!

Thank you to Linda Brennan, Cathy Brooks, and Kirstie Dean. You are all alternate thinks....capable of thinking outside-the-box and are curious about everything. You have always helped me keep my mind open.

For Coach Tim Dowling who began teaching me these concepts and skills as a high school swimmer. It took 25-years to get them fully incorporated in my competitive career but when I did they were like old, familiar friends. Thanks Coach for such a great start.

And, our final and never ending thank you is to Rich – husband and father – for his endless patience with all the dogs, training equipment all over the backyard, and all the long competition days. Without your support and endless encouragement, none of this would be possible.

Contact

If you want more information on Diane and Kathleen or want to check out their other books, DVDs and articles, please go to www.agilityandbeyond.com.